OF PACE

A Comprehensive System of Footwork
for
Stage Combat
by:
Payson Burt

4th Edition

Copyright © 1993, 1999, 2003 Payson H. Burt

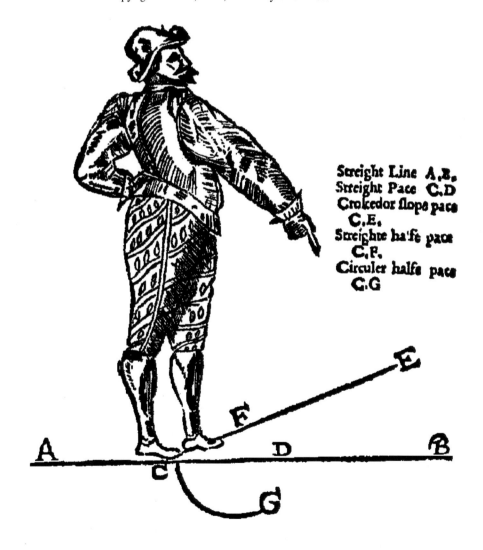

Illustration # 1: **Giocomo di Grassi** - Italy - 1570

Foreword

In the summer of 1988, I renewed my long friendship with Brad Waller after a six-year hiatus. Brad and I had started our careers in stage combat together and, since that time in 1982, had remained good, if not distant, friends. We immediately began spending time together fighting and researching, fighting and studying, fighting and drinking, and having the occasional brawl. It was wonderful to have him so near (as anyone who has been without a good friend close by in your field knows), and many ideas and explorations came to fruition. One of these labors we got very excited about, and this manual is the result.

Brad and I began looking at and experimenting with fighting in a circle as defined by the early Rapier work of the Italians in the mid 1500s. We then began to apply those techniques in the realities and priorities of Stage Combat, and we developed a system with which to teach. What we discovered was how much fun performing these new moves were to have in a fight, especially with the heavier weapons now becoming available through suppliers in this country. Further, we found that it injected all our work with newfound energy and specificity.

One of the obstacles we encountered while defining the terms in this system, was that there is no consistent system or vocabulary to break any steps down individually so that each movement had any number of definitions. Also, at the same time, distance became very hard to judge and fight notation a nightmare. Brad's enthusiasm, however, was overwhelming (if you have had the pleasure of working or studying with him, you know what I mean). Eventually using the manuals, our experience, and some creativity, we pounded out some definitions.

We began creating this system by going back to the old fight manuals of the 16th and early 17th centuries to find out how these steps were defined and taught. But which one? There were so many variations on footwork principles in those manuals that even if we concentrated on and emulated one single system, it would not only be incomplete, (for our needs as a system universal) but would be deeply rooted in the priorities of true sword fighting; e.g. our need in stage combat to <u>maintain</u> safe distance as opposed to closing distance for a hit. We therefore started with moves and terminology from one fight manual, Giocomo Di Grassi's True Art of Defense, and tried to find out a number of things:

1. *What do <u>all</u> the fight manuals have in common?*
2. *What do the old manuals have in common with footwork from the eastern martial arts and other system from around the world?*
3. *What works best when teaching students, or how can we simplify the principles of the above and make them practical and easily taught for stage combat?*

Also taking my personal experiences as a movement and martial artist, I knew that no matter how many systems there were in the world, the human body is made a certain way and those limitations are the common thread that binds every system of movement together. Therefore, what we needed to do was distill all the ideas, throw away the techniques that either complicated a definition or were repetitive, and start creating a new system from scratch.

What resulted was this system of footwork, rooted and inspired in those 16th century fight manuals, influenced by modern hindsight and by all systems from around the world, but simplified and easily taught to todays students of stage combat.

Lastly, another priority of the system was, as a certified teacher within the Society of American Fight Directors, to complement the present SAFD structure so that the techniques the society had labored so long to standardize would not be contradicted. To that end I have included, in the format of this essay, descriptions of basic linear steps in order to integrate them immediately into the system. This was written so that any beginning student could learn a complete footwork system, without contradiction, from this booklet. Therefore, starting with the introduction is a self-contained, comprehensive manual on footwork, which I have been using in class and choreography successfully for over 4 years.

Payson H. Burt
1993

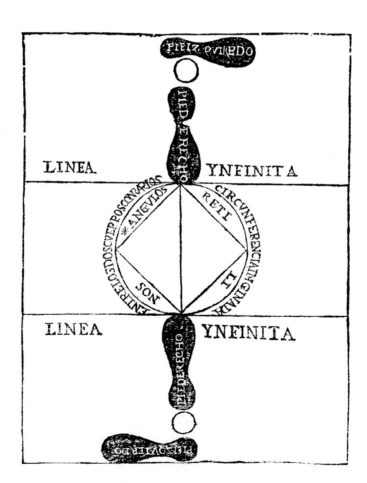

Illustration # 2 - **Narvaes** - Spanish - 1569

Acknowledgments

Brad Waller: *for without his initial inspiration this stone would never have begun rolling.*
The Society of American Fight Directors: *for creating a structure in which to learn and contribute to this art form.*
The Faculty of Temple University's Theatre Program: *For believing in me before I believed in myself.*
John Durning *and Durning Karate for photo help and the use of their studio space.*
Greg Dolph, Dale A. Girard, K. Jenny Jones, Colleen Kelly, Joseph Martinez, John Nelles, Richard Raether, Greg Ramsey, Julia Rupkalvis, Richard Ryan, Lewis Shaw and Robert Hamilton: *for their thoughts, opinions, and wisdom.*
Charles Currier: *for original diagrams.*
Jeff Jones: *for layout and computer help.*
Trampas Thompson: *for original artwork and graphics.*
Jayne Burt-Ozyildirim: *copyediting and proofreading*
Models: Trampas Thompson, Regan Forman, Michelle Ladd, and John Durning

To the Reader

The following manual is a work in progress. Many definitions and theories are in a developmental stage while others have changed with the discovery of what works and does not in the realities of stage combat choreography and teaching. As new terms and definitions develop, the nature and soundness of this text changes.

For instance, in the mid 1990s, the system stated that the forward foot in a Lunge from a Wide Stance needed to travel from the Forward 45 line to the Forward 90. But in drilling this Lunge with beginning students, I found that they would put too much energy going sideways instead of forward, which resulted in their forward knee and/or foot angling in – very bad for the knee. So, I modified this move to maintain the railroad tracks – keeping the Wide Stance. This was done to protect the knee – and it worked; the foot and knee stayed straight. Unfortunately, this resulted in an awkward and inefficient move – staying wide in the Lunge not only didn't allow the body to move forward as much as possible, but visually it was awkward – telling a confusing story to the audience.

So, looking at the advantages and disadvantages of these two opposite techniques, considering how beginning students of stage combat learn and develop, and the needs of theatrical illusion instead of tactical martial philosophy, I came up with a compromise – fixing the knee problem while visually making the Lunge look like it's primary intention is lengthening the stance to reach an opponent. The resulting solution is that the lunging foot – as the Lunge lengthens, will gradually move toward the Forward 90 line – but the goal is not to step on that line, rather as the Lunge lengthens, the feet narrow.

The reason I'm telling you this, is, because this problem with the knee arises as a result of a theatrical based modification to a sword fighting technique that has been around for centuries. The good news is that fixing this problem resulted in expanded explanation and increased specificity of foot placement in the Lunge section, but also it spurred the development of new sub-chapters in this book on **Hip Relationship** and **knee awareness**.

So, please bear with me as this system and its manual continues to evolve. I welcome your input and thank the many artists who have already expressed their opinions on this text.

Payson Burt   2003

Of Illustrations, Figures and Photos:

For ease in referencing, all images in this edition are numbered:

Illustration: a drawing or image from a fencing manual as an example of historical ideas concepts or positions. Also, modern drawings by my illustrator to show an overall body position in space.

Figure: is a graph, or feet images on a star.

Photo: well, you know what a photo is….

Contents

Foreword i

Acknowledgments iii

To the Reader iv

Introduction 1

I. The Basic Steps   5

    A. The Star and the Body   5
        1. The Star   5
        2. Stances   7
        3. Form   10
            Drills   15
    B. Movement   16
        1. Linear Steps   16
            a. Passing   16
            Drills   23
            b. Advance/Retreat   24
            Drills   26
            c. Lunging & Recovering   27
            Drills   32
        2. Off Line Steps   34
            a. Basic Traverses   35
            b. Variations on Traverses   37
            c. Changes in Traverses when in
                a One - Foot Forward Stance   39
            Drills   47

II. Period Specific & Combination Steps   48

    A. Volte and Demi – Volte   48
    B. The Half Passe   50
    C. The Hop   57
    D. Combination Steps   57
    E. The Sitting Thwart   61

II. Advanced Concepts and Drills   63

    A. Size of the Steps and Keeping Distance   44
    B. Teacher Notes on Drilling   76
    C. Keeping Distance while Fighting in a Circle   68

Glossary of Terms   84

Appendix 1 – Proximity   88

Introduction

In every method of defense there is a strong emphasis on footwork. In most systems there are very specific stances and placement of feet to guarantee a strong base and a mobile platform with which to evade, defend from, or launch an attack. Movement from that base must be specific in order to guarantee that the person's foundation does not disappear, leaving the performer without a solid base with which to move to the next step. The training reflects the nature of the weapon, and the ultimate goal is to be so versed in the basics of footwork that it frees the body from the restrictions of basic technique and propels it into the realm of accurate spontaneity.

T´ai Chi Ch´uan teaches the student to turn and step on very specific angles. These steps are on 90, 45, or 180 degree angles and are talked about in terms of the compass: North, South, East and West. The stances sometimes change while stepping, reflecting the unique nature of each posture; going from a T stance, similar to a foil fencing stance, to a more open front stance. The idea is to teach the student how to step from point A to B and still keep their center. Some of these transitions from one posture to another are easy and some are difficult; some postures may have you facing west and you must turn and step the long way around to the southwest. Any student of the art will tell you that no matter how difficult the transitions are, it must be made with as much precision and balance as one that is easy.

In the West, fencing and boxing are also very specific about their footwork. Muhammad Ali's "float like a butterfly" was all about dynamic footwork to confuse, misdirect and thwart any attack made at him while still having the power to direct an attack at his adversary. In fencing, the way to perform the advance and retreat are very specific, down to the instant one should lift and place the heel of the foot, as well as the more complex series of moves such as a Pattinando or a Fléche.

The ancient fight masters in the West, during the Renaissance, understood the importance for a system of footwork and came up with many systems that dealt with fighting in both a linear and circular manner. Generally, the concept of a <u>system</u> was the revolutionary idea that distinguished how combat was viewed before the Renaissance and after. Before the advent of scientific viewing of defense as a skill, the strongest and hardiest fighter won through mere force or from a variety of personal "tricks". However, with a system, a less hardy but more practiced man could defeat one who was stronger. This concept of a weaker man becoming victorious, by skill instead of strength, was a major reason the English, in particular, would resist these "newfangled" systems of fence.

Illust. # 3: From **Thilbaust** - Spain - 1628

Rapier play, however, did not have enough gestation time for the art to be standardized. It was in constant change, prone to improvement and innovation, and when there was finally some standardization, the weapon was not a Rapier, as we define it today, any longer. It had morphed into what we call the Smallsword around the 1700s and many of the circular fighting techniques were gone. To add to the confusion, there were still many schools and philosophies of fence. While the French developed Smallsword, many schools in Italy and Spain held on to the Rapier technique they had developed. The overall tendency was, however, for all the schools of fence to graduate to a more refined and economical use of the point and therefore towards an adoption of linear technique. Eventually, sword fighting became illegal and fencing became a sport. Swordplay was then further restricted to a narrow strip and, when that happened, even those feeble remnants of the Passe and Volte disappeared.

As the old ways of defense were forgotten and the new sport of fencing took over, the emphasis and specifics of circular fencing were also forgotten. This is unfortunate because no one master or school continued the art for its own sake like in the East, and this means we no longer have a direct way of learning this art. We can take some inspiration for learning footwork from the eastern martial arts that have survived more or less intact with masters that can teach its philosophy. In fact, many teachers of stage combat use eastern martial art footwork to help students learn and understand these same basic steps because they really do not have any other reference.

So, we see that specific circular techniques from the 16th century to the 18th century did exist; they simply were left behind for "more improved" technique. Now, we can easily look in any of the surviving fight manuals of the era to see and learn how it was done. In the long run, however, using the old fight manuals for our purposes in **stage combat** would be quite frustrating and inappropriate.

As Egerton Castle writes:
" *Such work would occupy a life time and fill a number of thick folios proving, moreover, quite as useless as those old and ponderous [manuals] which have been so religiously laid aside for centuries.*"[1]

Illust. # 4: From **Morozzo** - Italy - 1536

Just look at the cover art (you can see it completely on page 4); you see many angles and feet - a mystifyingly complex system which most actors would dismiss out of hand. Therefore, in the spirit of Egerton Castle, this system takes most of the basic, common principles from all the fight manuals, simplifies them, names them, makes them specific, and with specific modifications, makes it a comprehensive system for use in stage combat no matter with which weapon or in which historical period you are performing.

---

[1] Schools and Masters of Fence: Egerton Castle 1885 - Introduction

Before You Begin

It is important, for both teacher and student, to remember a few things before we start.

1. Although this system is inspired by the old fight manuals and uses some of the terminology of that time, this is a *completely new system* created for training students of **stage combat** in all weapons and/or applications, and the priorities and needs of this art form are completely different than that of competition fencing, historical fencing or sparring.

2. What this system is designed to do:
   A. Give the stage combat student a clear and simple understanding of *foot placement*. The better one understands and controls the placement of the foot, the easier it will be to match ones partner, maintain proportion and **keep distance**.
   B. Make stage combat instruction easier.
   C. Make fight notation easier and more standardized.

3. If you have had movement or martial arts training, you will see similarities to other systems - perhaps your own. Try not to make judgments. Remember the human body can move in only so many ways - there are bound to be moves and philosophies that repeat.

4. This system attempts to remove some of the mystery found in the martial arts (whether eastern or 16th century western), which were developed for completely different applications and student mind-set, by simplifying the concepts and making it easy to learn. Martial and competition arts are **tactical** by nature, while stage combat is **cooperative**. This means the pedagogy will be specific to developing consistency and predictability; two attributes that would work against you in a **tactical** situation.

5. This manual confines itself to a system of footwork that beginning actors may easily comprehend and master. Other concepts such as warm-ups, body alignment and center of energy are not covered extensively in this manual, but are valuable and should be addressed by the serious student.

6. This manual is intended only to supplement your training under a qualified teacher of stage combat. There are many qualified individuals and stage combat societies around the world who train and certify teachers who can help you complete the rest of your training.

Good luck and stay safe in your studies,

Payson H. Burt   1990

Illustrations 1 thru 4 - Examples of 16th and 17th century footwork diagrams.

◄ **# 1** - This is an illustration from Giocomo di Grassi's *True Art of Defence* written originally in Italy in 1570 then translated and published in England in 1594 by "IG Gentleman". It illustrates the steps as described by di Grassi: Starting with a straight line (A to B) he lists a straight pace, crooked or slope pace, straight half pace, and circular half pace. The text that describes these steps is recreated on page 29 in its entirety.

#2 ►

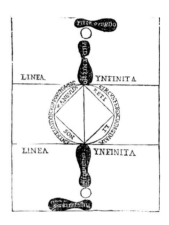

A Spanish system written by Don Luis Pacheco De Narvaes about 1569. Thilbaust, later in the next century, would beautifully illustrate the concepts that this manual pioneered. He based many of his techniques on this earlier work; it is one of the few Spanish manuals to survive today. Even in this earlier work, you can see a focus on angles and tangents that characterized the style of the Spanish.

◄ **Cover & #3**

This is a partial illustration from *The Academy of the Sword* by Girard Thilbaust, a French fencer and illustrator that chronicled the Spanish system of fence, as it existed around 1628. This is the center section of a set of 5 diagrams showing different sequences within the system. Sometimes called the "Mysterious Circle" you can see that this looks very complicated, and, in fact, it relied on mathematical angles and tangents that the rest of Europe neither understood nor imitated. They did, however, respect it, and Spanish duelists had the reputation as dangerous, cool-headed fighters.

 # 4 ►

This illustration is from Achilles Morrozo's *Opera Nova*. Considered by many to be the "grandfather" of the Italian school of fence that became predominate in the 1500s, Morozzo first wrote his work in 1536, and it was subsequently reprinted a number of times. This manual illustrates the early life of the Rapier and had enormous influence. This diagram shows one of two ways that Morozzo showed the position of the feet in his manuals. This star pattern is one, and the other was a grid floor in his illustrations that helped show the sometimes-subtle foot position in his manual. Examples of this grid pattern also show up in the illustrations of Fabris, and Saviolo – many of which you will see in this manual.

Chapter I: The Basic Steps
A. The Star and the Body

1. The Star

> **DEFINITION**
>
> **Star**: An imaginary series of 8 lines on the floor that radiate out from a central apex, beneath the combatant, consisting of 45 degree relationships like the points of a compass or lines of an asterisk. The points of the star indicate the variable planes of movement that a combatant may take.

a. First we start with a system of lines, which I call the **Star**:

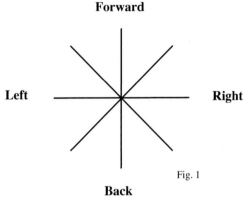

Fig. 1

You will notice there are linear relationships of 45 degrees and 90 degrees. I will refer to them in this way, but you can also describe the same lines using the degrees on a compass: North, East, West and South.

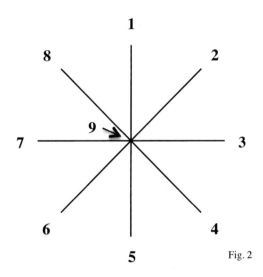

Fig. 2

b. I break the Star up into individual lines and name them thus:

1. Forward 90 or, North
2. Forward 45 right or, North East
3. Right 90 or, East
4. Back 45 right or, South East
5. Back 90 or, South
6. Back 45 left or, South West
7. Left 90 or, West
8. Forward 45 left or, North West
9. Center

Lines 1 and 5: Line of Engagement

Building your Star

The Space:

Although you may practice this system anywhere; your garage, basement, or at your crazy Uncle Harrys house, it is best if you have access to a space with a **sprung floor***; this work can be high–impact and a concrete floor can be very unkind to the feet and knees.

Also, having sufficient area in all directions is important so

*A sprung floor is a floor that absorbs shocks, giving it a softer feel.
Such floors are considered the best available for dance and indoor sports and physical education. They enhance performance and greatly reduce injuries.
Wikipedia

Photo # 1

you may perform multiple footwork without having to stop and reset yourself or your students. **Mirrors** are a plus so that you may see yourself and make adjustments in real time while your students can see the note your are giving them on their own body. Places such as dance or martial art studios.

If you take the time and trouble to build a Star, you also want to be able to use it repeatedly without having to continually rebuild it – so finding a dedicated space is important.

Supplies:

I find it best to use ½ inch "Spike Tape" to make the Star. You can use **chalk** for a very temporary Star or **paint** for a permanent one, but this tape is fast and relatively durable. Spike tape will last about a semester of constant use – If you have control of your environment, and are committed to this training, paint can be done once and forgotten about. Until that time, however, spike tape is the way to go.

Photo # 2

Spike tape, also known as gaffers tape, is a cloth tape used in stage and film production. It comes in a variety of colors and widths. It adheres to the floor nicely, but is not difficult to pull up. Because it is thin and made of cloth, it is easy to tear straight without stretching. Pick a color that stands out from your floor so that you may see the Star easily.

You can eyeball the construction of your Star. I do this all the time – at the beginning of a semester, for instance, where I need to build 3 or 4 of them quickly. Over time I became very good at judging the angles and you will too, but if you are doing this for the first time, I recommend you use some simple, inexpensive tools to ensure your angles are as accurate as possible. Things like carpenters squares or an architect's angle ruler. If you can, draw out the Star with chalk or pencil with these tools before laying down the tape. Accuracy is important in this system and if you are off on a line, you may be changing the foot placement and giving yourself or your student a bad template from which to drill.

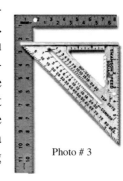
Photo # 3

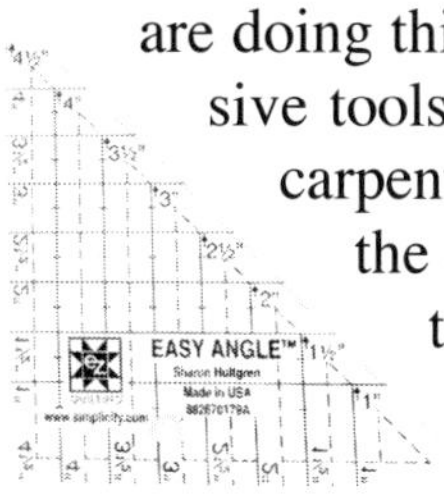

Photo # 4

Construction:

Most accurate: Using the square and angle tools, **sketch** out a Star. Then lay the tape over the lines as in the following paragraphs.

If you cannot mark your floor, do the following:

Photo # 6

Photo # 5

1. Pull the spike tape, drawing it to the full length of your extended arms – giving yourself some extra reach to pull the tape taught after tearing the end. This is an easy way to make all the lengths of the lines in your Star consistent. When placing your tape, be sure to pull it taught from the **ends** so that the tape does not "wander" off in a different direction as you place it on the floor.

2. Place your first line either North/South or East West. If your floor is wooden, you can use a plank line to start with. Pull the tape taught, place it on the floor and **mark the center** of this line.

Photo # 7

3. The next line placed is 90 degrees to the first one on the mark you just made. If the first line is North/South, then place the East/West line next, or vice versa. This is an easy angle to visualize, but if you need to, use the carpenters square – the longer the better. Again, be sure to keep the tape taught at the ends while placing it on the floor. Now you have 4 quadrants.

4. These next two lines are the challenge – holding the tape out at arms length, place it down in between the two lines previous, **thru the center** – creating a 45 forward and 45 back line. Use the angle template at first to ensure a good angle, but also step back and look carefully at the line to be sure you are perfectly **bisecting** the quadrant. It is very easy to wander on this line.

5. Do the same for the 2nd opposite 45 forward/back lines. It is common for one side of the tape to be correct in that quadrant, but the opposite end to be off – do not be afraid to stand back, look at it critically and, if necessary, pull up the end (or both ends) and reposition your line.

This is the basic Star – as we proceed through the manual, we will add other lines and marks.

2. Stances

> **DEFINITION**
>
> **Stance**: The foot positions and posture of the body that support the act of being En Garde.

American Heritage Dictionary defines a **stance** as: "The attitude or position of a standing person or animal, especially the position assumed by an athlete preparatory to action." Certainly getting ready to fight, whether boxing or sword fighting, constitutes an athletic event, so we will begin with these definitions. Since this system endeavors to simplify concepts, making basic technique universally consistent for the world of stage combat and separate the use of the feet from the upper body, I will start with two basic **stances**, and talk only briefly now about the different types of "ready" positions.

En Garde

> **DEFINITION**
>
> **En Garde**: The basic "ready" position of a combatant.

Although it is considered the ready position of sword fighters, you may be "on your guard", in all sorts of positions and situations and this is reflected by it's usage generally. So let us consider **En Garde** as a state of mind, as in "come En Garde". Meanwhile our work with **stances** will concentrate on positioning and posture.

For now we will concentrate on the following two **stances** and these will become the foundation of your work to follow.

a. Wide Stance

> **DEFINITION**
>
> **Wide Stance**: A stance that places the feet apart, straddling the line of engagement, allowing the upper body to face the opponent.

This would be a stance you could use for older weapons such as a **Quarterstaff**, **Broadsword** or early **Rapier**. This not only allows the upper body to face the partner but makes available the left hand for use with heavier weapons, or for left handed attacks and parries.

Start with the feet placed **shoulder-width apart,** and the center of the body over the center of the star. This is a **Neutral Stance**: Notice that the right and left 90 lines run through the center of the feet.

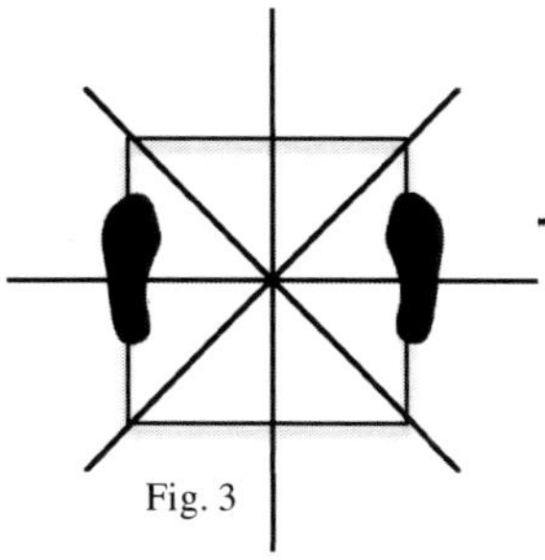

While standing in this stance, envision the following things:

1. Two lines running parallel to the line of engagement dividing your feet in half.

2. Note where these lines intersect with the Forward and Back 45 lines. These points will define where you will place your feet for a one-foot-forward stance. **Place a piece of tape on each spot.**

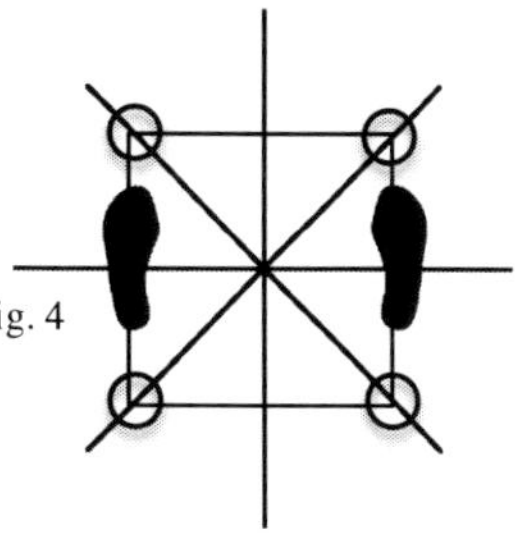

Fig. 3

Fig. 4

Illust. # 5

Fig. 5
Right foot forward
(RFF)

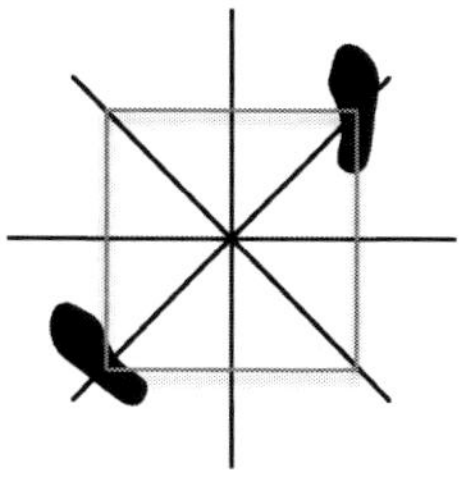

For a **Right Foot Forward Stance**, place your right foot on the Forward 45 right line while placing your left foot on the Back 45 left.

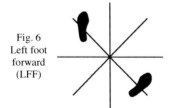

Fig. 6
Left foot forward
(LFF)

For a **Left Foot Forward Stance**, simply do the opposite: place the left foot on the Forward 45 left, and the right foot on the Back 45 right.

Width and Depth of your Stance

Width is in reference to the distance the two feet are from side to side, while the **depth** of the stance refers to their relationship forward and back. Be sure your stance has a balance of width and depth along the 45-degree line on which your feet are placed. It is basically a **square** stance.

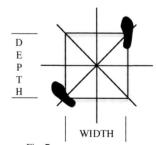

Fig. 7

Warning! Be sure to find your neutral stance with your feet **shoulder-width** apart. This means directly under your shoulders. If you increase this neutral stance even by an inch or two, it will geometrically increase the size of your stance.

- 8 -

Both legs are bent for a low center of gravity. Weight is 50/50. The knees should be just over the ankles, so when you look down, you can barely see your toes.

Angle of the Feet on the Star

In a **wide one-foot forward stance**, both feet are on one diagonal line, the front foot pointing directly forward and the back foot crossing the line at a 90 degree angle. The line should divide the back foot perfectly through the arch. The reasons for these specific angles will make themselves clear as we continue.

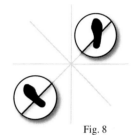
Fig. 8

b. Narrow Stance

> **DEFINITION**
>
> **Narrow Stance**: A weapon bearing foot forward stance keeping the feet almost heel to heel allowing the upper body to emphasize the weapon arm and turn away the torso.

This stance could be used for later European weapons such as late Rapier, Smallsword, and competition fencing. Here the upper body, the main target area in swords designed for thrusting, is made as small as possible by narrowing the feet. This allows the upper body to turn away from the attack and face a more perpendicular line to the partner, while bringing the point of the weapon into prominence. Within this general definition, there are choices on how to align the body (see the next section: **Form/Hip Relationship** for more information).

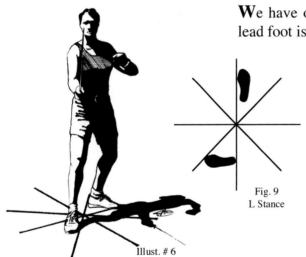

We have only one choice of foot position in this stance: The lead foot is always in consort with the sword-bearing arm.

1. The right foot is placed **next** to and parallel to the Forward 90 line.
2. The back foot is **perpendicular** to the Back 90 line with the heel just touching that line.
3. The relationship of the two feet is not quite heel-to-heel: <u>this is an **L** stance, **not** a **T** stance.</u> This stance is slightly more open than a strict foil stance for better balance. If your Star is using tape that is ½ **inch** thick – use that width to gauge your width. Theatrically, we do not need to be any narrower.

Fig. 9
L Stance

Illust. # 6

This stance, therefore, has **depth**, but very little **width.**

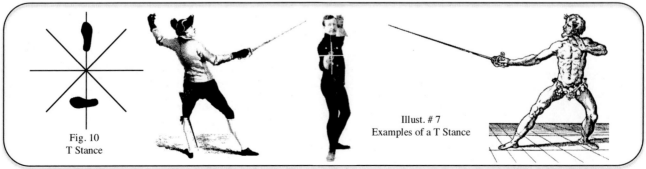

Fig. 10
T Stance

Illust. # 7
Examples of a T Stance

Finding the Depth of your Narrow Stance

You may find the **depth** of your stance in 2 ways:

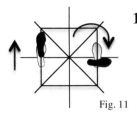
Fig. 11

1. Start in a neutral stance: shoulder–width apart. Pivot what is to be your forward foot parallel to the side 90 line it is on. Move your back foot forward so that the heel just touches the opposite side 90 line. Now pivot your body to face the new direction your feet are pointing.
   Warning! Be sure to have your feet under your shoulders: just like in the wide stance, just a few inches off will make your stance significantly deeper.

2. Start in a Wide Stance with one foot forward. Adjust your forward foot; while keeping it pointed straight ahead, move it sideways to the Forward 90 line stopping just next to it. Adjust the angle of your rear foot from 45 degrees to an angle perpendicular to the Back 90 line, and bring it toward that line so that the heel just touches.

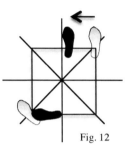
Fig. 12

Illust. # 8: **Sir William Hope** – Scotland - 1710

3. Form

Proportion

> **DEFINITION**
>
> **Proportion**: Agreeable or harmonious relation of parts within a whole; balance or symmetry.

roportion, in terms of usage in this manual, refers to the process of keeping one part of the body in **proportion** with the other elements of your stance and all movement you will soon learn. The very word **proportion** conveys a sense of spatial awareness and line of the body. For me, the interesting part of a fight is the breakdown of **proportion** when one side begins to lose. Of course, first knowing and being able to perform "the rules" is necessary in order to show it eventually dissolving.

The form may seem strict now, but having a specific set of parameters applying to all stances and movement at the basic level of training eliminates as many **variables** as possible in your fighting. The fewer variables, the more consistent you will be moment to moment while moving. Your knowledge of a good, neutral form will allow you to have a starting point with which to create the illusion of fighting well and, later in your training, "break the rules" in an informed way.

NOTE: For every rule, there is an exception. Everyone is built slightly differently, and for some, the parameters to follow might need to be adjusted. Studying under a competent teacher will ensure both safety and good form.

Hip Relationship

All movement comes from the hips or pelvic girdle. As you begin kicking out your forward foot on an advance, or passing your foot forward, the movement and intentions must begin in the hips. It is important that we have our hips correctly defined and aligned now, for it will affect all you do in the future. Also, as you work on the details of your form and increase the size of your steps, the hips will become very important in terms of placement and balance.

Using the star and the diagrams we add another symbol. This represents the hips and the direction they should face; envision the two hipbones on the front of the pelvis as the arrows.

Fig. 13

a. Wide Stance

With one foot forward, the hips are set at just shy of a 45 degree angle* in relationship to your partner or the Forward 90.

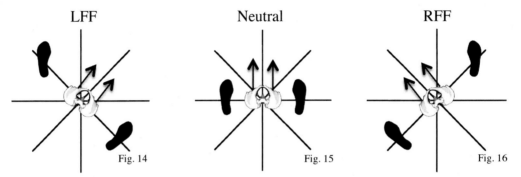

LFF — Fig. 14 Neutral — Fig. 15 RFF — Fig. 16

This alignment allows the upper body to comfortably face your partner and so use, in both a RFF stance and a LFF stance, the left hand. This also makes any transition between the two stances less extreme than if your hips are past the 45.

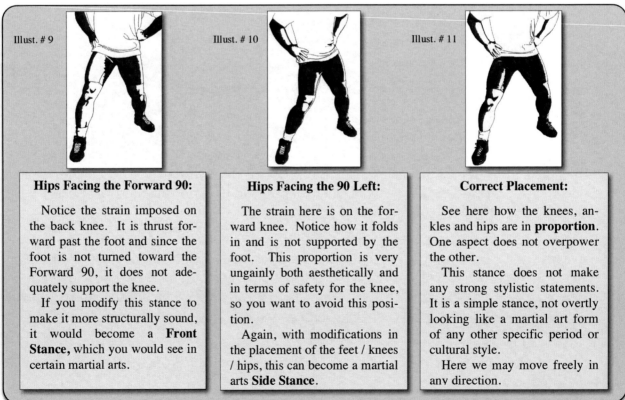

Illust. # 9 — **Hips Facing the Forward 90:**

Notice the strain imposed on the back knee. It is thrust forward past the foot and since the foot is not turned toward the Forward 90, it does not adequately support the knee.

If you modify this stance to make it more structurally sound, it would become a **Front Stance,** which you would see in certain martial arts.

Illust. # 10 — **Hips Facing the 90 Left:**

The strain here is on the forward knee. Notice how it folds in and is not supported by the foot. This proportion is very ungainly both aesthetically and in terms of safety for the knee, so you want to avoid this position.

Again, with modifications in the placement of the feet / knees / hips, this can become a martial arts **Side Stance**.

Illust. # 11 — **Correct Placement:**

See here how the knees, ankles and hips are in **proportion**. One aspect does not overpower the other.

This stance does not make any strong stylistic statements. It is a simple stance, not overtly looking like a martial art form of any other specific period or cultural style.

Here we may move freely in any direction.

*NOTE: The 45 degree reference is to be used only as a guide for you to find your own individual wide stance supported by the hips and protecting the knees. Many will find it more comfortable with the hips a few degrees more or less. It is more important to discover your particular angle and incorporate it into your form. A qualified instructor should assist.

The Upper Body

In a Wide Stance, the shoulders will not completely face forward - they will be ever so slightly asymmetrical. But there will be a stacking quality to the body as the legs are on one diagonal line, the hips are set at almost a 45 degree angle, and the upper body faces a little more toward the Forward 90 with a slight emphasis of the shoulder of the lead leg.

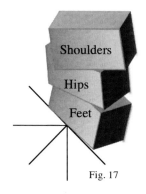
Fig. 17

b. Narrow Stance

Depending on the choice of angle for the upper body, which is affected by the use of the left hand, the hips may be positioned from the Forward 45, to just slightly past.

Some styles of late Rapier and Smallsword will use an **active** left hand, and, added to the fact we are using an **L** stance as opposed to a **T** stance, this will allow the *upper body* and *hips* to naturally face the Forward 45 left.

Illust. # 12

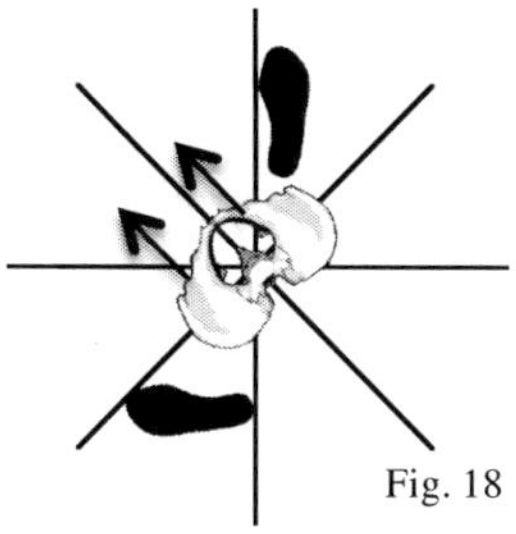

Fig. 18

Other styles of Smallsword have the hand positioned as in competitive fencing with a **passive** left hand (the hand up and behind the body, or on the hip), the upper body will face *more* to the 90 left and so will the hips.

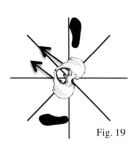
Fig. 19

This position is much more elongated than the previous Narrow Stance. There will be a feeling of opening the inner thighs; much like second position in ballet.

Illust. # 13

The Upper Body

The upper body in this stance is much more oriented over the hips whether you use a **passive** or **active** left hand. This puts emphasis on the sword bearing shoulder and arm, making them the leading part of the body while turning the chest and abdomen (the target areas for a thrusting weapon) away from the attack.

NOTE: These degree references are to be used only as a guide for you to find your own individual narrow stance supported by the hips and circumstance. Some will find it more comfortable with a very slight variance. It is more important to discover your particular angle and incorporate it into your form than to stiffly recreate any angle at the expense of your knees, balance or aesthetics.
Once again, a qualified instructor should assist.

Proportion of the Knees

It is very important for your knees to never overextend. Even if your feet are perfectly placed on the star, both in the wide stance and narrow, it is possible to lower your body too much and find yourself out of **proportion**. This is a very bad situation, and it may lead to serious strain on your knees. If you cannot look down and see your front foot without leaning your upper body forward, then you need to extend your legs until you can. You will see more of your lead foot than your back foot. Remember how you find your Wide Stance, always starting with the feet shoulder–width apart.

Illust. # 14

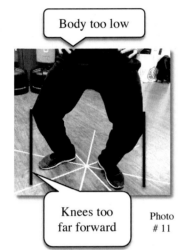

Body too low

Knees too far forward

Photo # 11

Use a full-length mirror and look at your profile while En Garde; your forward knee should be just over your ankle, or slightly beyond it over the instep. Your lower leg should be perpendicular to the floor or just **slightly** leaning forward. <u>If the forward knee is past the instep and the lower leg is leaning forward as in the photo at left, your body is either too low for your stance, or your feet are not positioned correctly on the star.</u> When you find your **proportion** for the forward knee, your feet are correct on the Star and you are not leaning onto your back leg; you should also find your back leg in proper **proportion**.

Illust. # 15: **Angelo** – England - 1765

The Big Picture

A system that deals in absolutes may have the attribute of being very specific, but chaining oneself to those absolutes can lead to inflexible technique. This section will continually address the long-term training applications: "The road ahead". Although it may not necessarily explain specific training, this section will be a review of what you just learned, a reminder of what is to come and how to keep the training thus far in perspective.

So far, we have examined two different basic stances and talked generally about some of the usages for each. The **Wide Stance** gives us the opportunity to use the left side of the body but makes the torso more open to attack, while the **Narrow Stance** pulls the vital organs away from an attack but makes the left hand less useful. With both stances we have explored simplistic **proportions** that ensure mechanical soundness and illusionary strength, or martial knowledge.

For example: within the **Narrow Stance**, we have looked at the single variance of using the passive or active left hand and how that choice can subtly change the mechanics of that stance. This is just one of the many different choices available when you are working within a specific circumstance or style. There are countless other types of stances used in martial arts both culturally and historically, and for every rule there is an exception or interruption. *The very nature of conflict is a world where intentions and form are not allowed to congeal as the opponent attempts to "disrupt" the other.* As an actor, you need to be able to show good form, which then allows you to show it dissolve in front of an audience. So, these two stances merely represent the foundation of all choices to follow in later chapters. Consider these, and the rest of the basic steps as a "phonetic alphabet"—exercises in placement—neutral choices from which all-future character and circumstantial variances will be defined.

These two stances will be used as landmarks that represent two extremes but may be used in conjunction with each other. Therefore, do not think of these stances as limited to one weapon or another. The specificity of each stance reinforced by the drills that immediately follow can help build an <u>awareness</u> of the body, feet and proportion. Conversely, it will inform you when you are out of proportion at any given time.

Acting application: there may be times in choreography where, within two moves, you transition from a Wide to a Narrow Stance. If that is the choice, it will have consequence, both for the actor mechanically and the moment dynamically. What is important, therefore, is that you are making a specific and informed choice.

Illust. # 16: **Sainct Didier** – France 1587

Drills

1. Stand over the star in a **Neutral Stance**. Feel what it is like to stand shoulder-width apart with the upper body straight. Bend the knees until you can barely see the outline of your toes over your knees if you look down without leaning forward. Do this until you can bend your legs in this **proportion** without looking.

2. From your **Neutral** Stance and with your legs bent, place your feet into a wide **RFF** and/or **LFF** stance; see if you can place your feet on the appropriate tape marks - do this until you can place them consistently without looking down. Do the same for the Narrow Stance.

3. **Leave the star** then return to it, so as to take away any physical "reminders" of where to place your feet and repeat exercise # 2. After succeeding a few times, do it faster, giving yourself less time to think about it. Remember your foot placement as illustrated earlier, keeping them both **deep** and **wide**. Maintain the proportion of your knees and hips.

4. In a **Wide Stance**, observe your hips pointing to the Forward 45. Try moving your hips to face straight ahead; feel what happens to your back leg. Next, move your hips to the Side 90 and observe what happens to your front leg. Now observe your upper body and try to force both shoulders to face forward, then relax it and see where it settles.

5. Repeat **exercise 4** with the **Narrow Stance** but experiment with the left hand and how the two different positions affect the alignment of the torso and hips. Go from an **active** left hand to a **passive** and experience the differences in hip placement between the two stances, keeping in mind what you experienced with the Wide Stance and how the hips and knees can either help or hinder the stance.

6. Stand in a **Neutral Stance**. Change to a **Wide** then to a **Narrow Stance**, pivot back to a **Neutral** stance. Are your feet still shoulder-width apart? Look below for the sequence.

You can play this exercise in any direction and in any order. You are testing whether or not your feet remain shoulder-width apart throughout.

COMMON MISTAKES

Bending the knees too much for the size of the stance.

Turning out the rear foot or turning in the forward foot.

Crossing the feet in the narrow stance. (4th position in ballet)

Placing too much weight on either leg; weight should be 50/50.

Hips not supporting the stance.

Leaning of the upper body either forward or back.

Figures 20 to 23

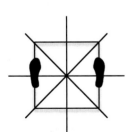 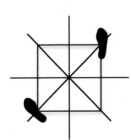 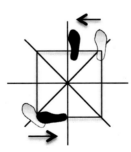 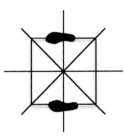

B. Movement

All but two steps in this system, whether linear or off-line, will have something in common: they are either **Posted** or **Recovered** steps.

> **DEFINITION**
>
> **Posted Step:** A step where one foot moves while the other remains stationary, or pivots, during the action. Performed in <u>Single Time</u>.
>
> **Recovered Step:** A step where both feet move. Most are performed in two counts; after the first step that initiates the movement; the recovered step usually will bring the person into a semblance of En Garde. Performed in <u>Double Time</u>.

1. Linear Steps

a. Passing

<u>The Single Passe</u>

> **DEFINITION**
>
> **Passe:**
> <u>Forward</u> - The placing of the rear foot in front of the leading foot (a walking step)
> <u>Backward</u> - The placing or the front foot in back of the rear foot.
>
> Both of these steps are **posted**.   (And yes, it is pronounced, "Pass".)

Before the development of modern linear technique (Advance, Retreat), the more natural action of "walking" towards or away from your opponent was used. This becomes most apparent when using a weapon made for two hands such as a **quarterstaff** or a two-handed **broadsword**. Also, when using a **shield** or a parrying **dagger** in your left hand a natural defensive position becomes left foot forward. The movement is simple as one foot "passes" the other. There are, however, several different ways to **Passe**. First we will look at a specific type of **Passe** that changes your Garde from one foot forward to the other.

<u>Changing the Garde - The Full Passe</u> - Wide Stance Only

> **DEFINITION**
>
> **Full Passe:** A type of Passe, forward or back, larger than a **Crossover**, that changes the alignment of the feet, hips and shoulders to a new En Garde in its execution.   This step is **posted**

While in a RFF Wide Stance, envision the following things:

1. 2 lines emanating out from the feet going parallel with the line of engagement. These are the "rails" your feet will follow while stepping, keeping your feet apart.
2. A 45-degree line coming out of the right foot, running parallel to the forward 45 left of the Star.
3. Your left foot will be placed where the 2 lines intersect.

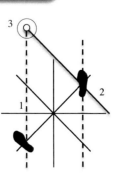

Fig. 24

Adding to your Star

Earlier, we added tape **marks** to the Star to indicate where you should place your feet for a Wide Stance. Now with the Full Passe, we must envision **longer lines** and they must be straight, so do this:

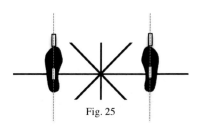

Fig. 25

Standing in a Neutral Stance, mark the center of your feet on the right and left 90 lines. It is easy if you mark the top middle of each foot.

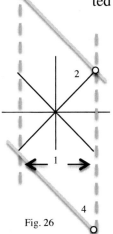

Fig. 26

You can use different color tape for your "railroad tracks", or the same but using a dotted line – as long as these new lines do not confuse the original Star.
I use dotted lines for the tracks.

Using the techniques from when you initially built your Star, add a pair of railroad tracks (#1) – going **past** the 45 lines of the Star. If you use a carpenters square again and are careful, you may find that your initial eyeballing of your stance is slightly off – this is a great time to fix that stance.

Next, we will add a **new** 45 line coming off the intersection of the right railroad track and the forward 45 line (#2). Using a carpenter's angle, take the line to the left until it intersects with the left foot railroad track (#3). This will give you an accurate point on which to place your left foot in a Full Passe Forward.

If you wish, add another 45 line off the **back** 45 left line to practice your Passe Back from your RFF En Garde (#4).

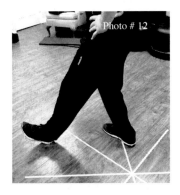

Now, move your back foot forward to that spot. <u>Reach with the heel</u>, and it will land first rolling down through the ball to flat. While your left foot moves past the posted leg, it will change from the 45-degree angle it was in En Garde, to straight ahead. You may circle the path of your step slightly in toward your posted leg to help maintain balance, but be sure to come back out to the target (#3).

As you **place** and roll your left foot <u>heel to toe</u>, two things will happen:

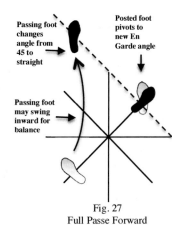

Fig. 27
Full Passe Forward

1. Your **hips** will shift to face the Forward 45 right line (see Hip Shift below).

2. Your right (posted) foot will shift angle so that it is parallel and on top of the Forward 45 right line.

When you are finished, you should be in a perfect LFF stance with all the same proportions as your RFF stance. This is a position of balance and power – one that is visually grounded telling an audience that the character is trained and ready for whatever happens.

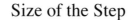

Photo # 13

pict of reaching with the ball of the foot

For a **Passe Back** from this position, while your **posted** foot is still on the Star (#2), simply step your left foot back to your original position. Even though you may bring the passing foot in toward your center, make sure it ends up on the intersection of the two lines. Again, the hip shift and foot pivot happens, but the reaching foot now leads with the ball of the foot, rolling down to the heel.

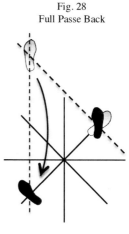

Fig. 28
Full Passe Back

Size of the Step

Step only as deep as is dictated by the intersecting lines you worked out earlier. Anything more or less deep will end up not being on the 45-degree line needed to ensure a good proportion in your **Wide Stance**. Coincidentally, the step will be approximately one-foot length past your posted foot. This will be your **standard** step.

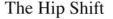

Illust. # 17: **Capo Fero** - Italy - 1610

The Hip Shift

The primary use for these steps forward or back is to change your guard from one foot forward to the opposite. After the step has been made, we must be ready for any step that follows be it an Advance/Retreat, another Passe or an Off Line step. This means your new stance must be as precise and balanced as possible. Shifting the hips and adjusting the rear foot allows you to retain your form while doing this.

This shift happens just at the last moment of the step, and the posting foot adjusts through the energy of the hips. This will give specificity to the action of the shift and allow you to quickly finish the move in way that grounds you.

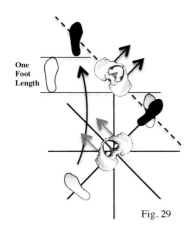

One Foot Length

Fig. 29

The Standard Step

> **DEFINITION**
> a.) The established middle landmark for any step within the structure of three sizes of steps: Shallow, Standard and Deep.
> b.) The neutral execution of any step.

As we continue to define terms, **standard size** will be seen more often. The standard step becomes a **landmark** for you to recreate consistently, understanding that later in the process this allows you to actively choose a shallower or deeper step than your established **standard step**. The better you know this landmark you are developing now will heighten your total body and spatial awareness.

The Crossover
Wide and Narrow Stances

> **DEFINITION**
>
> **Crossover:** A type of Passe, forward or back, smaller than a Full Passe, that does not change the alignment of the feet, hips, or shoulders in its execution. This step is **posted**.

This version of the Single Passe is called either a **Crossover**, or sometimes simply a **Passe**. Here, the objective is to maintain the present En Garde and **not** shift the hips or upper body. As in the Full Passe, you step forward with the heel, and backward with the toes.

Wide Stance

The faded image under the left foot is for measurement purposes only – the heel line is the key – do not reposition the foot while stepping– keep the alignment throughout the step and land it at a 45 degree angle.

Illust. # 18

Begin by stepping forward with the left foot–heel first–and discover when the hips begin to become engaged. This means when the hips begin to turn naturally; this is generally the size of your step. Measure your step specifically (one half foot length from the tip of your posted foot) and perform it without any shifting of the hips or upper body.

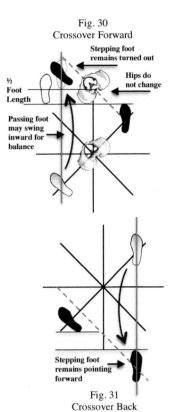

Fig. 30
Crossover Forward

Stepping foot remains turned out
½ Foot Length
Hips do not change
Passing foot may swing inward for balance

Stepping foot remains pointing forward

Fig. 31
Crossover Back

This would represent the **standard** size step for a Single Crossover both forward and back.

Be careful not to let the stepping foot go off your **rails**. This is particular to the Wide Stance where the passing foot will have a tendency to narrow the stance on the completion of the step.

Narrow Stance

The Crossover is made for the Narrow Stance, where the philosophy of keeping the sword bearing shoulder forward as you walk forward or back is very clear. The extremity of the posture and foot position demands this sort of step, or else we end up waddling to and fro – not very dashing. There is no **Full Passe** in the Narrow Stance, only the **Crossover**; which is defined and measured just as in the Wide Stance with the only differences being in width of the stance, and the angle of the back foot.

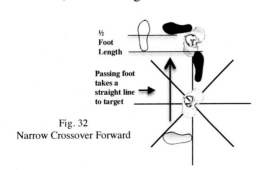

½ Foot Length
Passing foot takes a straight line to target

Fig. 32
Narrow Crossover Forward

Illust. # 19:
Angelo – England - 1765

With both the Crossover forward and back in the **Narrow Stance**, you can feel the tightness of the step. The shoulders, feet and hips follow a direct and focused line with very little deviation. Working in the Narrow Stance usually means a refinement of form and movement, and that should be reflected in the specificity of this step.

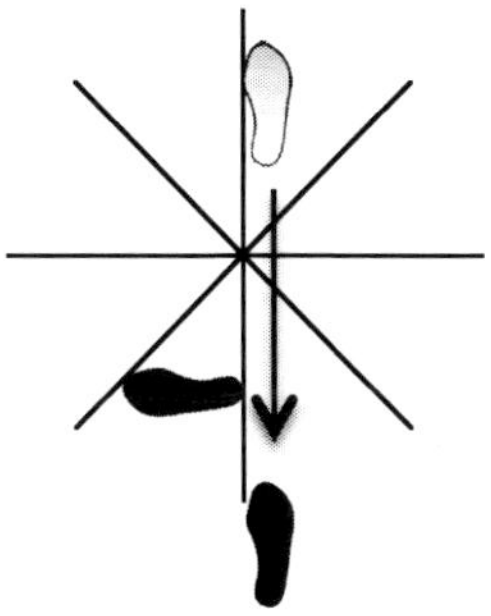

The Crossover can be stopped and reversed easily, or also continued on into a **Double Passe**. As such, it then becomes a **transitional step**, and the first half of the next step we will learn - the Double Passe forward and back.

Fig. 33
Narrow Crossover Back

> **DEFINITION**
> **Transitional Step:** Any step that is part of a larger whole, but has a definite beginning and end; usually will have multiple options at its completion.

Size of the Step

A Crossover is defined by the rotation of the hips. Even though the foot is not placed on an intersection of lines as in the Full Passe, you can still place your foot with specificity. Using the graphs and your Star, staying aware of when your hips start to turn, and placing – not falling into your step, you can work out where your foot plants for the Standard step. Learn this well. The philosophy is that if you find yourself having to step **shorter** or **longer**, you have built awareness through your training about the size of each step, you are able to adjust the size consciously. This concept will be explored more fully in later chapters. For now, therefore, train these two steps with the specific sizes that have been laid out.

Multiple Passing

The Double Passe

> **DEFINITION**
> **Double Passe:** The combination of two passes, either forward, or back.
> Both these steps are **recovered**

A Double Passe looks like you are simply taking two steps toward or away from your partner. However, subtle details are in play. In this step, as in a **Crossover**, we are not switching to a different En Garde, but **maintaining** it throughout the action. Each passing foot maintains the angle it had in En Garde, and the hips do not shift between steps.

The back foot will **not** turn and face the partner—it will keep the angle it had in the En Garde all the way through the 2nd step and, when complete, will be in the same relative position from which it started.

> The first half of the Double Passe (a single Passe or Crossover) has now become a **transition** step.

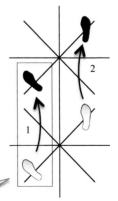

Fig. 34
A Double Passe Forward from a Wide Stance

The Double Passe - Wide and Narrow Stance

Wide Stance

Starting from a wide En Garde with your RFF (pos.#1), your feet will be positioned on one diagonal line: the Forward 45 right, and Back 45 left. The **standard** first step in our Double Crossover Forward is <u>one half-foot length past your posted foot</u> in size. Reach with the **heel** for both steps. Step #2 brings us back to a right foot forward En Garde (position # 2). Notice that this is simply an En Garde with both feet on the same line (Forward 45 right and Back 45 left) as in position #1.

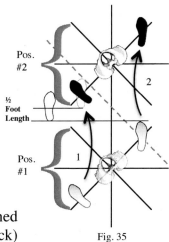

Fig. 35
Wide Double Passe Forward

This step is **asymmetrical** with step #1 smaller than step #2.

We are basically repeating the Crossover that we learned earlier and continuing in the direction (forward or back) to recover our En Garde in the appropriate stance.

Going backward, remember to step with the toes first, and to keep the alignment of the feet the same as in En Garde.

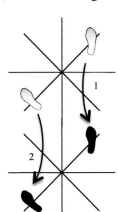

Fig. 36
Wide Double Passe Back

Illust. # 20:
Capo Fero – Italy - 1610

Narrow Stance

This version is performed and measured the same way as in the Wide Stance. The only differences are in the width of the stance and the angle of the feet.

Remember when your feet are narrow; the passing foot keeps the **90-degree** angle to the line of engagement throughout the step. This is also true of the Double Crossover Back, where the right foot passes and keeps the toes pointed straight ahead.

When going backward: whether wide or narrow, reach with the ball/toes of each passing foot.

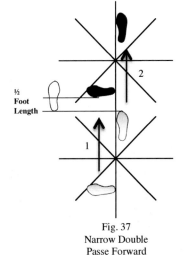

Fig. 37
Narrow Double Passe Forward

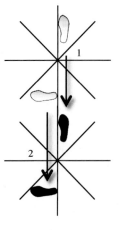

Fig. 38
Narrow Double Passe Back

Form

In all the steps covered, it is important that the movement is centered in the hips and not in the upper body. Any leading of the upper body or shoulders whether forward or back will mechanically create a moment where the performer is off balance. This will also **visually** weaken the action; the step will be out of **proportion** and therefore should be regulated to a character or circumstantial choice instead of a habit.

Be clear as you move that you are either **maintaining** or **changing** your stance; you cannot do both. If you are **changing** En Garde, the hips and shoulders move *specifically* to a new angle. If you are **maintaining** En Garde, be sure to emphasize that maintenance and eliminate any unnecessary shifting of the hips or shoulders.

At no time should you fall into a step. The feet should glide over the floor with no stomping, hopping, or dragging. This is most difficult in the **Full Passe**; you will need to lower your center of gravity by bending your posted leg while reaching with the passing leg. This must be timed out and done in **proportion**. This skill will be addressed more fully in a later chapter.

The Big Picture

The system is beginning to establish landmarks: Stances that are **wide** or **narrow**, steps that are **shallow**, **standard** or **deep**, and form that is very specific. *These are not absolutes.* Right now we have **two** landmarks for our stances; eventually we will have more. As we move, we are working now to **maintain** that stance while stepping a specific size with no extraneous movement. Clarity, specificity and consistency are what we are trying to develop. Along with these attributes will come awareness of when you are *not* in your stance, or *not* performing your standard step.

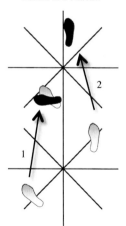

Fig. 39
Dbl. Passe Forward adjusting from a Wide Stance to a Narrow

Later down the road, we will explore how to consciously **change** your stances from wide to narrow or vice versa, or deepen your step at a moments notice. Once we get to that point, you will begin to experience the freedom of varying your choice for an upcoming move in choreography, a character or circumstantial moment, or simply to compensate for a mistake made by you or your partner. But that will come later.

Once again: and it does keep coming to this - the important thing for now is that you are *stepping with specificity and awareness*.

Illust. # 21: **Morozzo**
- Italy - 1536

Drills

Full Single Passe

1. After figuring out where your feet are placed - both forward and back, place a piece of tape on each spot. From a RFF stance, Passe Forward; watch and make sure you place your foot over the tape. Be sure you stay in proportion. Now Passe Back and see if you return the left foot to its place over the Back 45 left line. Do this until you can place your feet without looking and perform this on either side.

2. Play with the level of energy on your hip shift. Try being very aggressive in your shift while waiting till the last moment to perform it. While doing this, be sure to only shift as far as you need - if your stance narrows and/or your hips point more to the Side 90 lines, you will work much harder than necessary. Practice your shifts and make sure you are going from 45 degree to 45 degree.

3. Observe your upper body/shoulders while you perform the Passe. There should be no pushing or leading with the upper body; it should be very relaxed as you step. The natural shoulder leading should fall into place while you passe. Once again, if your shoulders reflect a large one-side orientation, your shift will be large and unwieldy.

4. Be careful of your knees as you explore this step and shift. As you shift, your forward knee must remain in line with your ankle. Your forward foot should point straight ahead while your back foot rests at a 45-degree angle. Any variation of this form is an indication that one aspect of the step is out of proportion. (See page 10 for more explanation about the relationship of the foot, knees and hips).

COMMON MISTAKES

Stepping too deeply or too shallow.

Allowing the feet to leave the "Railroad Tracks".

Shifting the hips too far from side to side.

Shifting the hips too early.

Pivoting the feet too much or too little.

Allowing the knee of the forward leg to fold inward.

Ending the Passe with too much weight on either the front or back leg. Weight should be 50/50.

Full Double Passe

1. Continue your exercise with the placement of the passing foot on a full passe. This time, however, do not pivot the feet or shift the hips. Double Passe Forward, then back, working on the size and placement of each step. Try to move smoothly forward and back. You should end back on the Star.

2. Use the momentum of the 1st step to propel you into the 2nd step witch takes you back to En Garde. Try not to fall into the first step: keep low and reach with the stepping heel. Be sure to end with your weight 50/50.

Making the first step too small.

Shifting the hips and upper body on each step.

Falling into the first step.

Crossover

1. Find the size of your Crossover and mark it with a piece of tape. Work until you can consistently place your foot with accuracy. Work forward and back in both a Wide and Narrow Stance. Work on performing the Single Crossover smoothly in two ways.
    a. Finish with the weight 50/50, wait a beat then go back or forward to En Garde. The second movement should be smooth without any leaning or the body.
    b. This time, reverse direction and return the passing foot back to En Garde. Try to bounce back immediately but make sure you achieve your 50/50 weight distribution accurately - then smoothly change direction. Do this forward and back.

Making the first step too small.

Ending with too much weight on either the front or back leg. Weight should be 50/50.

Losing En Garde (shifting the shoulders)

In the Wide Stance, narrowing the rails.

Double Crossover

1. Step smoothly through both steps without bouncing or leaning. Feel your weight rolling smoothly through the posted foot as you transition the weight from the 1st step to the second. When you return to the Star - are your feet back in position?

2. Feel the asymmetrical nature of the step, and the syncopated rhythm that results. The first step is smaller than the second. Try to emphasize this fact in the rhythm by not lingering in the first step. This will give the illusion that you are aware that the first step is a moment of vulnerability (a transitional step) and that the emphasis is in returning to an En Garde as quickly as possible.

Performing both steps with equal rhythm.

Leading with the forward shoulder.

b. Advance/Retreat

> **DEFINITION**
>
> **Advance**: Sometimes referred to as the "fencing step". The leading foot steps forward, followed by the trailing foot.
>
> **Retreat:** The rear foot steps backward, followed by the front foot.
>
> Both of these steps are **recovered**.

The Advance and Retreat are the most recognizable steps in sword fighting. These are the steps you see when watching fencers compete. They were a later development in the art of swordplay as the focus shifted from a two handed style of sword fighting (whether using two hands on the sword or using a second weapon in the left hand) to a lighter, more point-oriented style that used the sword for defense as well as offense.

Advances and Retreats are designed to maintain the sword bearing shoulder toward the partner while keeping the main target area for thrusting as far away as possible from attack. These steps are **recovered** and therefore are performed in two counts.

Since these are steps that were designed for a Narrow Stance, we will learn them from that perspective first and then adapt the steps to the Wide Stance.

Advance

Narrow Stance

For the first part of the Advance, look down at your forward foot, and in **one swift move**, replace the tips of your toes with your heel. This means you must pivot your foot upward, bringing your toes up and placing your heel on the floor. At the same time, push forward with your back leg through the foot along the side. The forward foot will end with the heel on the ground and your toes up in the air while your stance ends up extended with both legs almost straight.

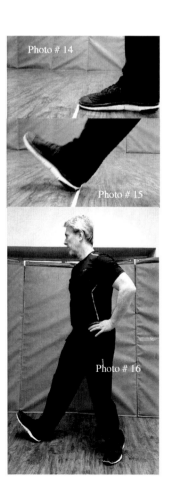

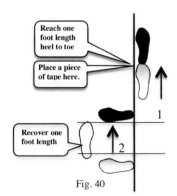

Fig. 40

In the next move, two things happen **simultaneously**:

- The toes of the forward foot come to the ground.

- The left foot **recovers** forward, the same distance (one foot) and therefore maintains **proportion** for your En Garde.

Adding to your Star: Place a piece of tape at the tip of your toe. This will give you a target to place your heel upon.

Retreat

Photo # 17

The Retreat is performed exactly the opposite of the Advance by simultaneously reaching with the **ball** of your back foot exactly one foot length while pushing backwards with the **front** leg.

In the second part, the **heel** of the back foot comes down as the forward foot **recovers**.

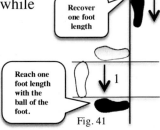
Fig. 41

It is harder to gauge the size of this step: because of this, the Retreat is usually learned and performed smaller than the Advance. You can, however, do a few things to make sure this does not happen:

1. Measure out the length of your foot, place a piece of tape where your back foot should be, then take some time and actually look behind as you practice reaching with your foot to get a feeling of how large the step needs to be. Then perform the Retreat and check out your accuracy after you step.

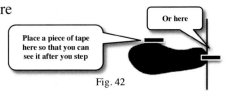
Fig. 42

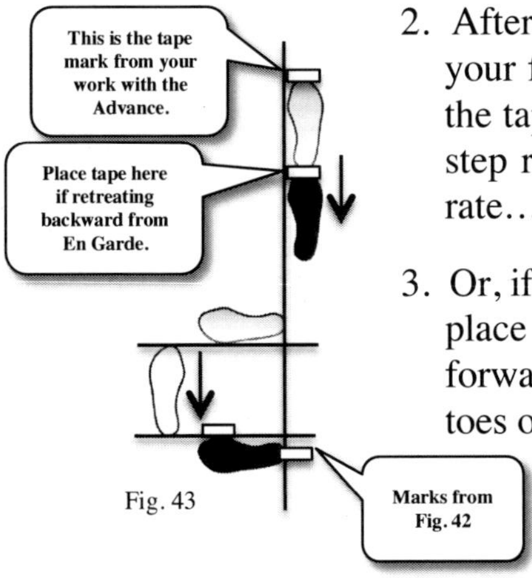

2. After moving forward on the Star with an Advance, a Retreat should bring your forward foot back to its original placement on the Star. You can use the tape you placed earlier at the front of your foot to see if your recovered step returns you to the tape mark. Just make sure your recovery is accurate…

3. Or, if you are retreating from an En Garde on the Star, while in your Stance, place a new piece of tape at the **heel** of your forward foot. Observe your forward foot **after** the Retreat to see if your reach and recovery bring the toes of that foot to this tape mark.

Fig. 43

Wide Stance

In the Wide Stance, the Advance and Retreat are performed the same way except for the width of the stance, and the angle of the back foot. Both feet, however, must be kept apart. Use the "rails" on your Star.

The back foot measurement for both steps is even harder here because of the angle of the foot, but you can still place tape at the toe.

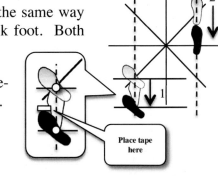
Fig. 44
Retreat in a Wide Stance

Form

Be sure the Advance emanates from a combination of pushing with the rear leg and reaching with the front leg. Watch out for over indicating with a large kick. This can eventually be a nice cue for your partner, but for now try not to rear back or over indicate the kick while going forward.

In the Retreat, do not throw your back foot upwards as you reach. With both the Advance and Retreat, since you are only reaching one-foot length, the step will not be overly large – yet.

Hip Relationship

You should maintain the same hip relationship throughout the Advance or Retreat without changing the angle. If you are in a Wide Stance (illustrated), maintain your hips just shy of the 45-left line. If in a Narrow Stance, maintain whatever angle you are using for that stance. If your hips are misaligned during the move, a similar situation arises as illustrated on page 9.

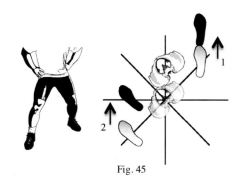

Fig. 45

Glide Along the Floor

With both the Advance and Retreat, make sure you are not hopping, which is an indication that, in the Advance for example, you are kicking too hard with the forward foot and pushing upward too much with the rear leg for the size of the step. Make sure you do not dip which is an indication of stepping too deeply without kicking out and pushing enough. You want the waistline to "glide" along the floor. Do not drag the trailing foot (dragging the back foot on an Advance is common) and, in a Wide Stance, do not allow the feet to close in onto the line of engagement.

Drills

1. Begin Advancing across the floor. Put your awareness into:
   a. Moving exactly one foot length
   b. Gliding across the floor
   c. Recovering your Garde exactly - if you do not, after you are finished a number of Advances, your stance will have either deepened or become shallower.
   d. In a Wide Stance, maintain the rails.
2. Practice the Retreat in the same way.
3. Vary from Advance and Retreat - Mix them up liberally. Focus on equal weight distribution at all times.

Mixing

At this point you can begin to alternate Advance/Retreats with Passes. Certain combinations will have unique challenges.

1. Advance/Retreat in a Wide Stance with the right foot forward. Full Passe forward or back, then continue Advancing/Retreating with the left foot forward.

2. Perform the following Combinations:
   a. Passe Forward, Passe Back, Advance.   b. Passe Back, Passe Forward, Retreat.
   c. Double Passe Forward, Retreat.   d. Double Passe Back, Advance.
   e. Double Passe Forward, Advance.   f. Double Passe Back, Retreat.

3. **Mix and match** Advances, Retreats, Full Passes, Crossovers and Double Passes as much as you can.

COMMON MISTAKES

Stepping too shallow or too deep, resulting in hopping or dipping.

Recovering your Garde too much and reducing the depth of your stance

Recovering your Garde too small and expanding the depth of your stance

Ending with too much weight in the direction of the technique.

Allowing the "rails" to narrow in a Wide Stance.

Leading too much with the left side when the left foot is forward.

Not completing each step as you proceed i.e.: rushing into the Advance before finishing the Passe.

c. Lunging and Recovering

The Lunge

> **DEFINITION**
>
> **Lunge:** The "extended" leg position used as a method of reaching the opponent on an attack. To lunge, the leading leg extends forward in a long step, while the trailing leg stays in one place.
>
> This is a **posted** step.

Illust # 22:

Even though the concept of reaching out linearly in an attack was most probably used for centuries, the Lunge as a specific and defined technique did not appear (at least in writings and common practice) until the beginning of the 17th century. This coincided with the rise of linear thrusting technique as well as the use of the Advance and Retreat.

The forward Lunge follows the same concept of the Advance—maintenance of the sword bearing arm forward and keeping the thrusting target (the upper body) as small and as far away as possible from any potential attack. As such, it is performed much the same way as an Advance, but with one important distinction: It is a **posted** step instead of a **Recovered** step. The **Recovery** is performed as a separate step. In all other ways, however, it maintains the concepts we have established with the Advance in terms of hip relationship, upper body form and the action of the forward foot in the first part of the step.

Finding the Size

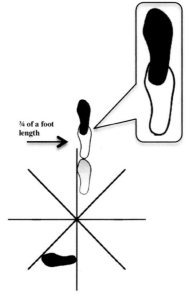

Fig. 46

Beginning in a Narrow Stance, advance your forward foot just as you would in an Advance, replacing the toes with the heel. Do not recover your back foot, but straighten the back leg and keep the foot planted firmly on the ground. Note where the ball of your right foot is on the floor, mark it, and advance the front foot a second time so that the heel is at that spot. The **depth** of your lunge is now 1¾-foot length. The forward knee is bent so that the knee is directly over the ankle and the upper body is straight up and down with no leaning forward. This will be your **Standard Lunge**.

NOTE: Two full foot lengths may be appropriate for those who have fencing training or martial arts or whatever has helped them develop strong legs. A beginner will be better off with a standard Lunge of only 1¾-foot length. Studying with a competent teacher will ensure both safety and good form. Whatever size you choose; make it consistent.

A qualified teacher should assist.

Form

The Lunge moves the body and hips linearly forward by **deepening** the stance. The movement primarily comes from the extension of the rear leg forward and is facilitated by lifting the leading foot and placing it firmly on the ground forward of its previous position. The forward foot should not initiate the movement but is almost forced to move by the extension of the back leg, which is moving the body forward. Be sure not to "rear" back and overemphasize the kicking aspect of the leading foot, although judicious use of this kick is a good way to focus the energy forward, and can eventually be a nice stylistic or circumstantial choice. The front foot should glide along the floor and land heel first. In a **Standard Lunge**, the weight distribution is about 60 percent on the forward leg with no leaning forward with the upper body.

After finding your **Standard Lunge**, be sure of the following:

A. The forward foot should travel and end completely straight and parallel to the forward 90 line. Be careful not to allow the foot to "sickle" inward.
B. The forward lower leg is perpendicular to the ankle, so that the knee is bent and over the ankle, **not past the toes**. To check this, look down over your knee without leaning forward and you should just see the outline of your foot around the knee.
C. The back leg is straightened *completely*, but not hyperextended.
D. The back foot is firmly on the ground. Be sure not to allow the foot to roll over to its side. This foot is your "anchor" as it grounds your movement.
E. The upper body is straight up and down without any leaning forward.
F. Just as in the Advance, the **hips** and **shoulders** maintain their angle, unchanged from your En Garde. The combination of the hips turning toward the Side 90 and the foot sickling inward will put the forward knee in danger.

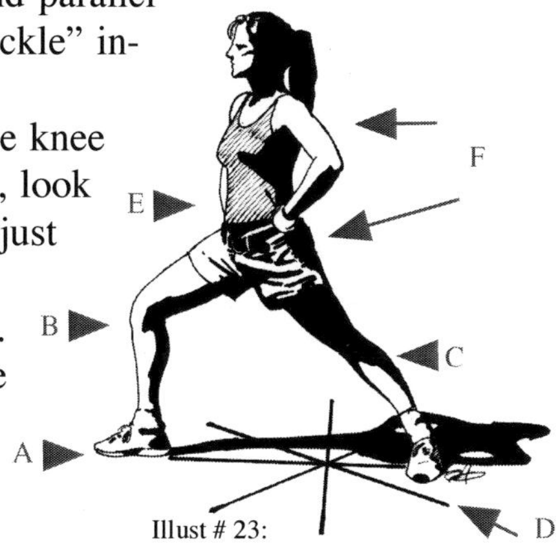

Illust # 23:

Narrow Stance

The Lunge was developed as the En Garde became narrower and as such, is very easy, efficient and natural to perform in this stance. The Lunge simply kicks straight out, and the forward foot follows the line of engagement (the Forward 90 line).

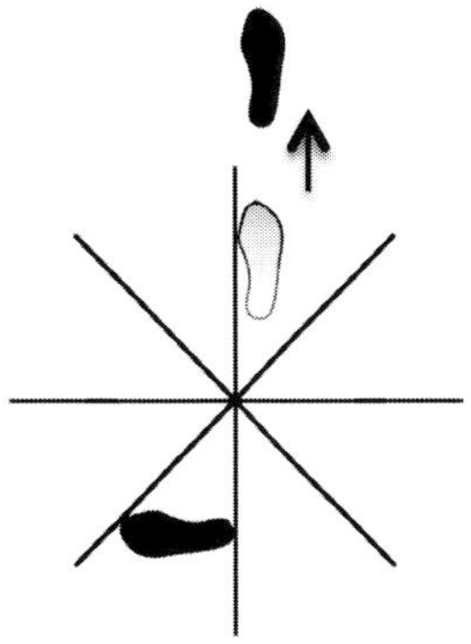

Fig. 47

Wide Stance

In the Wide Stance, valuable leg length is lost when maintaining the **rails**. So, we narrow our feet slightly – the 1st step narrows the stance by ½ foot width. The second step (1 ¾ deep) is also narrowed by ½ a foot width. The final position of the front foot is closer to the forward 90 line, but not next to the line as in the Narrow Stance.

*Be especially aware of the hips and forward knee in this Lunge. A tendency will be to turn the hips toward the Side 90 and allow the forward knee to fold inward (Hip Relationship; section A).

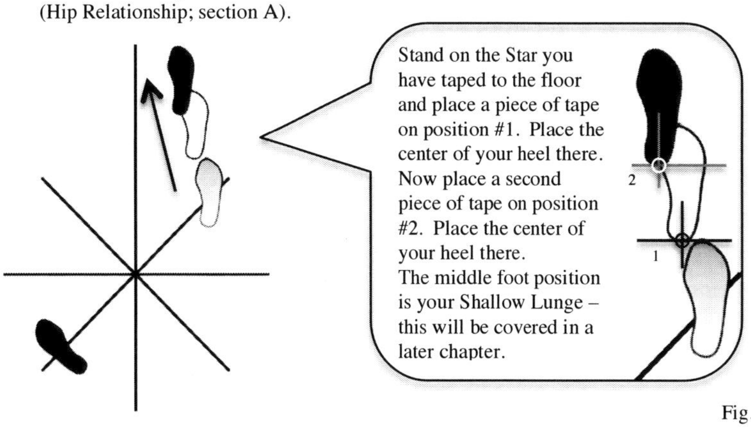

Stand on the Star you have taped to the floor and place a piece of tape on position #1. Place the center of your heel there. Now place a second piece of tape on position #2. Place the center of your heel there.
The middle foot position is your Shallow Lunge – this will be covered in a later chapter.

Fig. 48

The Recovery

> **DEFINITION**
>
> **Recovery Backward:** To arrive at an En Garde position from a lunge by bringing the forward foot backward. This move **creates** distance.
>
> **Recovery Forward:** To arrive at an En Garde position from a lunge by bringing the rear foot forward. This move **decreases** distance.
>
> Both these steps are **posted**. (screwy, aint it?)

The Recovery is a specific move to bring the body back to En Garde from a Lunge. The Lunge and Recovery *combined* would constitute a recovered step (like an Advance), so don't be too confused with these steps being posted. The Recovery is performed the same from both a wide and narrow stance.

Recovery Backward

The forward foot simply pushes off and comes back to its original position before the Lunge. <u>At the same time, the back leg bends</u>, reestablishing En Garde. Notice here the amount of movement in the hips - they move back identical to the Lunge from which it Recovered.

Recovery Forward

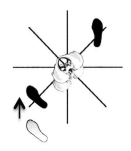

Here, the back leg bends and the rear foot comes forward. Notice that although the back foot moves forward the same distance as the Lunge; the hips (and therefore the body) move very little. The back leg moves from its extended position back under the body, changing the weight distribution from 60/40 back to 50/50. The Lunge moves toward your target, and the Recovery Forward maintains that ground taken.

Recovering in Proportion

Be sure, as you Recover, that you move the recovering foot proportional to your Lunge. If you do not, your En Garde will be affected; either your stance may deepen or become more shallow. This is, once again, very much like when performing an Advance or Retreat; the recovering leg is as important in the execution as the specificity and size of the first part.

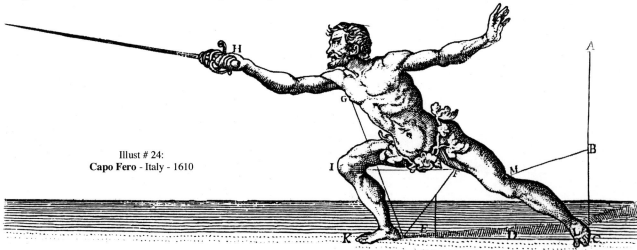

Illust # 24:
Capo Fero - Italy - 1610

The Lunge with a Thrust

Although this system attempts to separate footwork from specific attacks or defensive actions, the Lunge is so linked to the execution of a thrust attack that an examination of this move is necessary at this point. You can, of course, perform a cut while Lunging (all that you are doing in a Lunge is moving the body forward while maintaining the sword bearing arm forward), but the attack with the point and the concept of this execution is basic to the performance of almost any attack with a sword.

En Garde and Extension with the Sword

The holding of your weapon is the last ingredient of En Garde. While in En Garde with a sword, allow the shoulders to relax, the arm to bend at the elbow with the elbow in front of the body 1½ fists distant. The forearm is parallel to the ground, which means the wrist is at the same level as the elbow. The wrist may be either palm up (**Supinated**) or palm down (**Pronated**).
The point of the sword is above the hand at the level of your collarbone. The overall line is one of being open and elongated - try not to have any sharp angles.
The extension simply drives the point forward with the arm straightening behind it.

25

Do the following:

a) From En Garde, **extend the sword arm forward**. This action is lead by the hand (or tip of the sword); not the elbow or shoulder, and is isolated from the rest of the body: no leaning forward or turning of the upper body. The arm extends straight out so that the wrist is in line with the shoulder.

b) **Lunge**. The straightened arm pulls the body into the Lunge. This is not to say you lean into the Lunge as a beginning move, but that the body immediately follows the arm after it extends. The lunging action is still propelled by a combination of the kicking of the forward foot and the extension of the back leg.

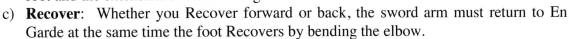
Illust # 26:

c) **Recover**: Whether you Recover forward or back, the sword arm must return to En Garde at the same time the foot Recovers by bending the elbow.

d) **Coordination** - Both the sword arm and the recovering foot should start and stop together; they should move in **Proportion**.

That Darned Knee!

Oh! That forward knee that either overextends past the foot or folds inward! The folding happens especially in the **Wide Stance**. Compensate by opening the inner thighs (like in second position in ballet).
Finding your Standard Lunge will not ensure good foot/knee position; you can be fooled kinesthetically if you rely solely on the feeling of your legs and how separated they feel. The result is that you spread the legs like you remember, but the foot does not step out enough. **The lunging foot must be trained to step out proportional to the opening of the legs.** This is where the specificity of your size using your **feet** is important to understand and recreate consistently. The size of the step will inform the legs how spread they should be.

27

28

The Big Picture

For now, whenever you Lunge, your ending position should be a **Standard Lunge**; with all the elements of **form** discussed earlier, and your arm extended. Depending on your stance, and the nature of the weapon, you might find your left hand in the following positions

1. Wide Stance, left hand **active**: The left hand is reaching forward - just past the elbow - ready for a counter attack, or shifted to another line for the same reason. It is very prominent so as to be as useful as possible in both attacking and defending.
2. Narrow Stance, left hand **active**: Here the left hand is at the elbow or closer to the body; to reach more would to turn the body and expose it as a target. It is also more defensive in nature; ready to deflect an attack that may get beyond your sword.
3. Narrow Stance, left hand **passive**. From an elbow back position, the arm shoots back into any number of attitudes; from straight out with palm upwards to a very formal extension parallel to the back leg with the hand open, or stays on the left hip as in saber fencing.

While the rest of the body is isolated; adhering to the form set up earlier, explore the possibilities with the left hand. As long as you are not turning the upper body or leaning, the left hand can be very expressive and tell an interesting story.

Look at the different Lunges presented below: See the different attitudes each puts forth. Each is performing a Lunge, but what specific choice out of a **Neutral Lunge** has been made to reach further or use the left hand? Observe all the varied leg, knee and hand positions, and how the body is used. This is where we are headed in our study of these movements. What specific isolated physical choices are being made to create a "picture" to the audience?

So, although the natural tendency is to lean forward or turn the torso in the execution of a Lunge in order to reach a little farther in the attack, we are **eliminating** those choices for now so that we may add them in later consciously. Therefore, our "Neutral Lunge" is the foundation for all these choices to be explored later in our study.

Illust # 29:
Examples of different types of Lunges

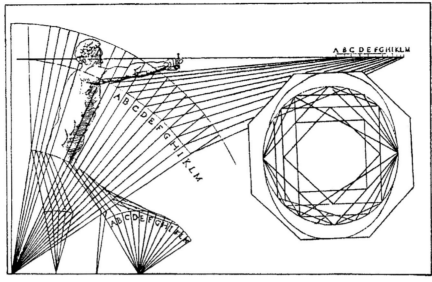

Illust # 30:
Agrippa – Italy - 1568

Drills

1. Practice lunging, recovering forward and back in both the wide and narrow stances. Concentrate on the following:
   a. Form: Hip and shoulder alignment, back leg extended and foot firmly on floor with no rolling over, forward foot straight ahead.
   b. Size: Make you lunge consistently a **Standard Lunge**. This is very important in the long-term applications when we examine distance.

2. Extend with the Lunge then Recover; the action should be 3 distinct movements.
   One - extend
   Two - Lunge: Count it out in two even counts.
   Three - Recover forward/back. The arm and foot are performed in one count and in **proportion**.

Mixing

Alternate Advance/Retreat, Passes and Lunges
Certain combinations will have unique challenges.

1. Perform the following combinations:
   a. Advance / Lunge / Recover
   b. Retreat / Lunge / Recover
   c. Lunge / Recover fwd. / Advance
   d. Lunge / Recover back / Retreat
   e. Lunge / Recover fwd. / Passe fwd
   f. Lunge / Recover back / Passe back
   g. Dbl. Crossover fwd. / Lunge / Recover fwd
   h. Lunge / Recover fwd. / Lunge

2. Mix and Match Advances, Retreats, Full Passes, Crossovers and Lunges as much as you can.

COMMON MISTAKES

Inconsistent size.

Not executing the Lunge by extending the rear leg.

Not finishing the extension first.

Extending by leaning or turning the body.

Recovering the foot too much or not enough.

Not completing the action of a step before continuing into the next.

Not ending steps other than a Lunge in a 50/50 weight distribution.

After a Double Passe Forward, Lunging too deeply.

Of Paces.

It is to be knowen that the feete moue either streightly, either circulerly: If streitly, then either forwardes or backwards: but when they moue directly forwards, they frame either a halfe or a whol pace. By whole pace is vnderstood, when the foot is carried from behind forwards, keeping stedfast the forefoot. And this pace is sometimes made streight, somtimes crooked. By streight is meant when it is done in the streit line, but this doth seldom happen. By croked or slope pace is under-stood, when the hinderfoot is brought also fore-wardes, but yet a thwarte or crossing: and as it groweth forwardes, it carieth the bodie with it, out of the straight line, where the blowe is giuen.

The like is ment by the pace that is made directly backwardes: but this backe pace is framed more often streight then croked. Now the midle of these backe and forepaces, I will terme the half pace: and that is, when the hinder-foote being brought nere the foore-foote, dothe euen there rest: or when from thence the same foote goeth forwardes. And likewise when the fore-foote is gathered into the hinder-foote, and there dothe rest, and then retireth it self from hence backwards. These half paces are much vsed, both streit & croked, forwardes & backewardes, streight and crooked.

Circuler paces, are no otherwise vsed than halfe paces, and they are make thus: When one hath framed his pace, he must fetch a compase with his hin-der foote or fore foote, on the right or left side: so that circuler paces are made either when the hinder-foote being setled before doth move likewise on the right or left side: with all these sort of paces a man may moue euerie waie both forwardes and backewardes

Straigt

C 2

Excerpt from:
De Grassi
Italy
1570

- 33 -

2. Off - Line Steps

> **DEFINITION**
>
> **Traverse:** Any foot movement that takes the combatant off-line.

Stepping off line is to move away from the line of engagement. This can be done for two reasons: 1. In **defense**: to dodge an attack, or 2. In **offense**: to move around a shield or weapon, finding vulnerable angles in an opponent's Garde where the body can be attacked or the balance taken. Generally, **Traverses** represent on older form of militaristic combat before single civilian combat refined linear technique and thrusting. The weapons were often heavier or double handed, and popular tactics included overpowering, pushing, and grappling; this is in contrast to false edge parades, elegant Lunges, ripostes, and other lighter techniques representative of later linear civilian sword work. In order to successfully overpower an opponent, or attack around a Garde, finding the best **angle** was an essential attribute and fighting manuals in the first half of the 16th century – and earlier – are thorough in their explanation of closures, in-fighting, and wrestling techniques.

Most martial systems of the later 16th century, as thrusting techniques became more refined, still followed this basic military philosophy, including weapons like the Rapier. The transition from weapons handling in the battlefield to the streets of the city was still very new. In many places techniques overlapped; a major concern of late 1500s England, in particular, was that gentlemen were spending too much time training for single combat and not enough on training as a soldier. George Silver went as far as saying that these individuals were being unpatriotic because they were leaving England weakened in case of war[2].

This evolution away from circular fighting proceeded slowly because of many factors: First, simply because evolution tends to be slow; people have an inclination to maintain tradition, as illustrated in England. Also, the technology was limited; the sword blades were still comparatively thick, heavy and brittle – regulating the use of the sword to primarily an offensive weapon and leaving the defense to a shield or secondary left handed weapon. Lastly, when one is faced with danger, rules fly away, instinct takes over and two individuals fighting for their lives in a field or courtyard, I believe, would use any advantage and angle to win the fight - even in the 18th century during the reign of the Smallsword. For me, therefore, a clear theatrical choice could be to have a character go from the linear to the circular as a means of illustrating his rise of desperation and loss of proportion.

This is not to infer that **Traverses** are simply out of proportion or represent moments of desperation. Dual weapons styles like Rapier & Dagger are full of finesse yet still relied heavily on Traverses. The Spanish continued to teach stepping off line well into the 18th century. Getting around a shield or, later in the century, a Guardia as opposed to rushing straight through became a science and the Spanish system of fence emerging in the late sixteenth century represents this growth to its extreme.

Fig. 11: **Agrippa** - Italy - 1568

---

[2] George Silver - Paradoxes of Defence: Weakened in two ways: One, in terms of education: If one is spending time learning to play with rapier, then that is less time working with the true weapons of war and therefore wasting time and energy. And two, rapier fighting was more deadly - a puncture wound more often led to infection and death as opposed to a good laceration with an edged weapon so the unpatriotic gallants were weakening England through unnecessary death

a. Basic Traverses

The general term *Traverse* is broken down into 3 <u>specific</u> steps.

Thwart • Cross • Slip

We will start our learning of the Traverses in a Neutral Stance. This will show the symmetry of the steps before performing them in an asymmetrical stance.

Left and right are in reference to which direction the *body* is moving in relationship the star. The basic premise while moving off line, for now, is that you are responding to a single focal point (partner), not multiple. The **Forward 90** therefore, is the constant reference to the position of your partner.

1. The Thwart

> **DEFINITION**
>
> **Thwart:** A **posted** or **recovered Traverse** on the <u>Forward 45 degree</u> line ending with the legs open.

Thwart Left
Posted

Thwart Right
Posted

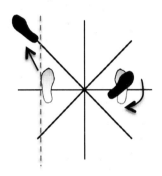

Recovered

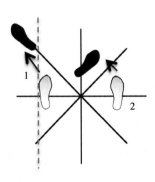

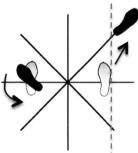

Recovered

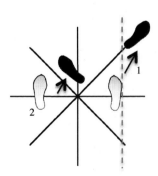

Notes:

A. The posted Thwart is a Lunge on a Forward 45 line. The size and form should repeat the performers standard forward Lunge.

B. The Recovered Thwart is an Advance on a Forward 45 line. The size and form should repeat the performers Standard Advance.

C. In both posted and recovered Thwarts, the front foot is on, and pointing in the direction of the line it is stepping upon, the hips are at the appropriate angle (see hip relationship).

D. The back foot should pivot so that it has a perpendicular relationship with the line of the Lunge/Advance – almost becoming a Narrow Stance on the 45 line.

2. The Cross

> **DEFINITION**
>
> **Cross:** A **posted, passing Traverse** on the <u>Forward 45-degree line</u> with the legs ending crossed. The passing foot travels in front of the posted foot.

Notes:
A. Make sure the step is completed in balance - the body weight is 50-50.
B. The step should only be made as deeply as is needed to clear the body off line while keeping both legs bent. See how the feet line up with the dotted line. (For more info, see "size of the steps").
D. The back heel may rise off the floor.
E. Turn the stepping foot inwards so that the toes are pointing at the partner.

3. The Slip

> **DEFINITION**
>
> **Slip:** A **posted, passing, Traverse** on the <u>Back 45-degree line</u> with the legs ending crossed. The passing foot travels behind the posted foot.

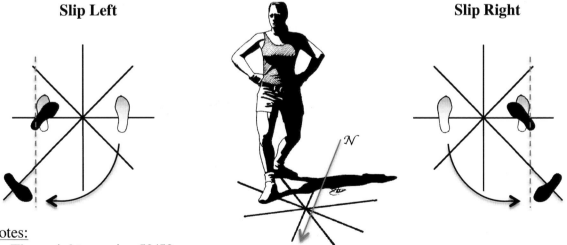

Notes:
A. The weight remains 50/50.
B. The posting leg may pivot and adjust as is needed.
C. Be sure to step out on the 45 line; it is easy to "work too hard" and compass farther than you need.
D. As with the Cross, step only as deeply as is needed to clear the body off line. Notice the dotted lines.   (For both C & D, see "size of the steps")

b. Variations on Traverses

basic rule to follow is that the Thwart and Cross are **forward** steps and the Slip is a **backward** step. They are always on the 45-degree mark. In other words, Thwarts and Crosses are on the Forward 45 lines, and only Slips are on the Back 45. However, we can modify the nature of the steps by including more information on angle and direction.

1. Thwarts

Supply the angle and direction, and we can simply place the feet on another line ie: Thwart to the 90 (Right), or Thwart to the Back 45 (left)

Thwart to the 90 Left

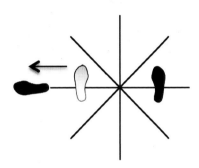

Thwart to the Back 45 Right

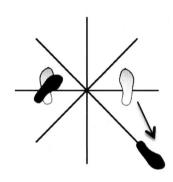

Notes:

A. As a posted step, it is very important to perform theses steps specifically: Pivot from the hips and shift the posting foot, support the right knee, not letting it either fall to the inside line nor let it extend over the front foot (see "hip relationship").
B. These can be used as a traditional avoidance.
C. The Thwarts to the back are now **increasing distance**.

Fig. 12: **Fabris**- Italy - 1606

2. Crosses

Cross to the 90 Left

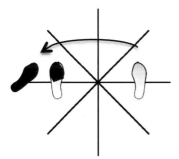

Cross to the Back 45 Right

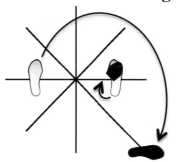

Notes:

A. These steps are difficult, but are excellent balance exercises.
B. The posted foot may adjust as the step is executed, and the heel will rise.
C. The Crosses to the back are now **increasing distance** – and the foot cannot face the partner.

3. Slips

Slip to the 90 Left

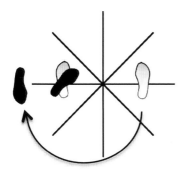

Slip to the Forward 45 Right

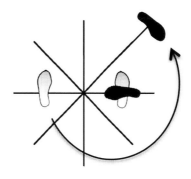

Notes:

A. The Slip is retiring in nature, but a Slip to the Forward 45, for instance, can be a very effective displacement-attack. **This step decreases distance**.
B. Take care – it is very easy to "work too hard" on these moves and overstep.
C. The posting foot must make an adjustment so the knee remains safe.

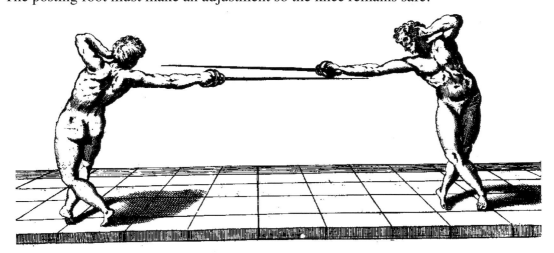

Fig. 13: **Fabris**- Italy - 1606

c. Changes in Traverses when in a One-Foot Forward Stance

The Neutral Stance gives the beginner a sense of symmetry and order in this system. I have found it best to learn the off-line steps in this environment, and then graduate to an asymmetrical (one foot foreword) stance. When this happens, the steps change slightly in nature. This section will address those changes in specific terms.

Certainly the type of guard will dictate what is an effective move and what is not. With a Wide Stance, the logic was to present the upper body and left hand to be useful in the fight, making Traverses possible both to the right and left. Passing was popular and guards were designed for both an offensive stance (RFF) and defensive stance (LFF). Therefore in a LFF stance, a Slip Left would be deemed a logical and efficient move. Even from an RFF En Garde, Traverses to either side are still reasonably efficient because of the width of that stance.

In the **Narrow Stance**, the logic was to turn the body away from danger and present the right shoulder forward as the sword assumed the dual responsibility of offense and defense. Because of the narrowness of the stance, some of the off-line techniques become illogical. It is a truism that linear techniques had, by the time Smallsword was in fashion, nearly taken over the art of sword work. Generally speaking, Slips to the left became less common as did Thwarts and Crosses to the right. However, the opposite of those steps, Crosses to the left and Slips to the right, became very popular and efficient, as we shall see in section two.

1. Wide Stance

All diagrams are with a right foot forward stance.

Thwarts -Notice in terms of final foot placement all these posted Thwarts are performed as a Lunge with the foot and knee supporting the body in that direction.

Thwart Right

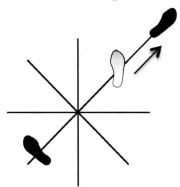

Since both feet are on one diagonal line, the right foot simply steps further along that line in a Lunge. In terms of distance, you do not move forward much.

Thwart Left

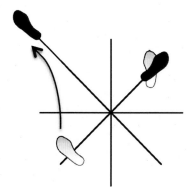

Here the action of the feet are more like a Passe Forward with the left foot passing and stepping diagonally on the Forward 45 left. The right foot must pivot to provide the correct line of the lunge. The moving foot comes slightly into center before stepping on the line.

- 39 -

Thwart to the 90 Left

Thwart to the 90 Right

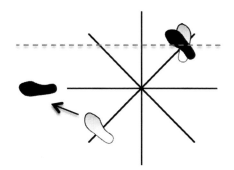
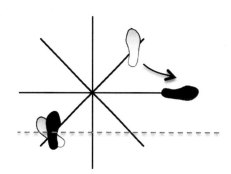

In the **Thwart 90 Right**, notice that the right foot does not go back to the same plane as the left foot but only to the Right 90 line. **This step increases distance**. When stepping to the **left**, the foot comes forward to the 90 line, but not to the plane of the right foot – **decreasing distance**.

Note: In all these steps, observe how the posting foot either pivots to create the correct line in a lunge (for thwarts) or releases on crosses and slips.

Crosses

Cross Left

Cross Right

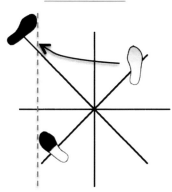
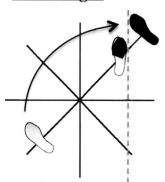

Notice here that the **Cross Right** is a much tighter move than the **Cross Left,** which has much more space between the feet and knees. The Cross Right, when starting from a RFF stance, should find the right knee firmly supported by the inside of the left knee.

Cross to the 90 Right

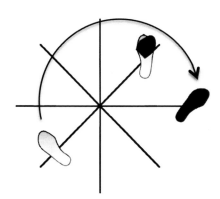

With the right foot forward, the **Cross to the 90 Right** is not a reasonable step to take unless it is a **Finito**, or running away move. This step is much more useful and reasonable from a LFF stance, as you will see in the next diagram (imagine this and the next diagram reversed with the left foot forward).

Cross to the 90 Left

Here we step on the **Left 90** and because that line is forward of the posted foot, it is a much more reasonable step. **This step increases distance**.

Fig 14: **Sutor** - Germany - 1612

Slips

Slip Left   Slip Right

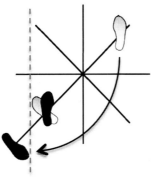 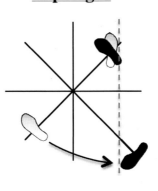

With your right foot forward, all the Slips to the right will be much easier to perform. This is just the opposite from the Cross. The Slip Right is much more open, while the Slip Left must compass all the way around the posting foot.
Note the release of the posting foot.

Slip to the 90 Left   Slip to the 90 Right

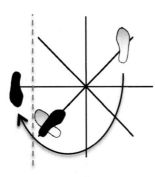 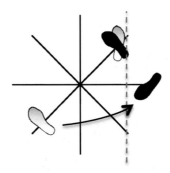

The Slip to the 90 **Right** finds the left foot coming only to the Right 90 line, <u>not</u> up to the posted foot. The Slip to the 90 **Left** finds the right foot <u>past</u> the posted foot on the 90-Left line. The Slip Left **decreases** distance, while the Slip Right **maintains.**

Slip to the For. 45 Left   **Slip to the For. 45 Right**

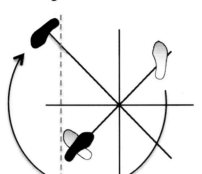   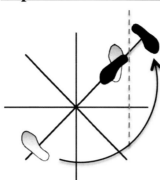

The Slip to the Forward 45 Right ends with the left foot on the same Forward 45 line as the right foot (looks like a backwards cross right). The Slip Left compasses all the way around the posted foot to the line. This is an enormous move with the RFF and is usually used when the left foot is forward. <u>Note</u>: The posting foot must release for these steps.

Hip Relationship - Thwarts

Two things to observe here:
1. Since you are basically performing a Lunge, no matter what line you are stepping on, your hips should be offset 45-degrees to whatever line your Lunge is on.

Thwart Right   Thwart to the 90 Right

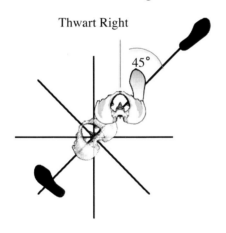   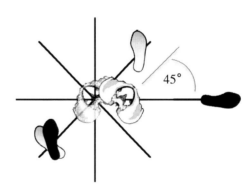

2. You can see how the rotation of the hips supports these steps. If the energy of the move is balanced between the step of the forward foot, the pivot of the back foot, and the hips, the step can be both quick and precise.

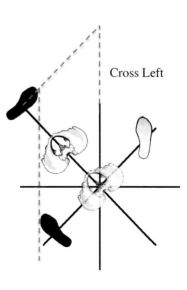

Cross Left

The Cross

The goal of the Cross is to **continue to face** the imaginary partner. You can use the Forward 90 line as a reference. With that goal, the crossing foot turns in to **point toward the partner**, and the hips try to **maintain** their angle. This will become more difficult as the angle increases – ending with the Back 45 that will turn away from the original angle, but only as much as is necessary to facilitate the feet and your balance.

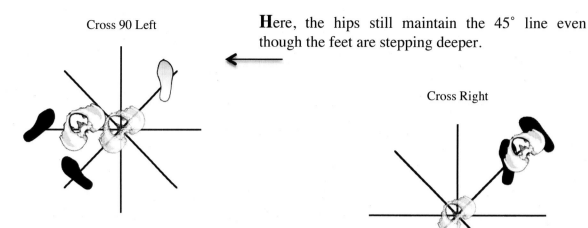

Cross 90 Left

Here, the hips still maintain the 45° line even though the feet are stepping deeper.

Cross Right

Even though the Cross Right travels in the opposite direction, the goal is to keep the hips on that 45° angle (although they will shift clockwise slightly). ⟶

The Slip

With the Slip, the body is rotating <u>away</u> from the line of engagement and so the hips will follow and turn in response to this.

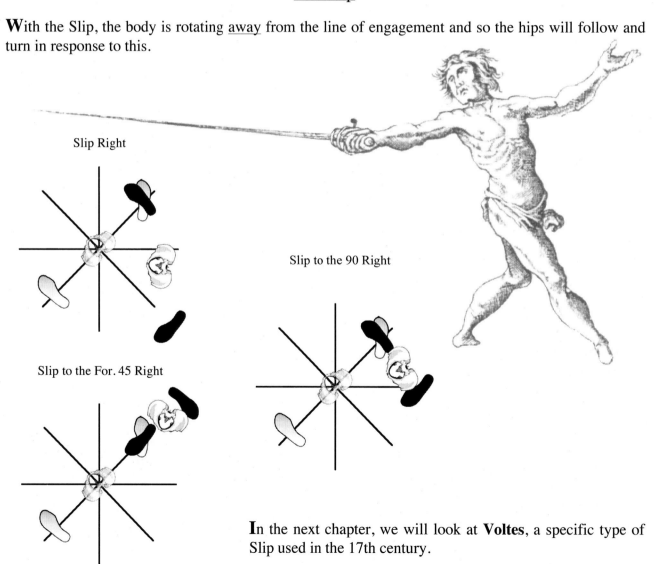

Slip Right

Slip to the 90 Right

Slip to the For. 45 Right

In the next chapter, we will look at **Voltes**, a specific type of Slip used in the 17th century.

2. Narrow Stance

Even though the nature of the Narrow Stance is linear, off-line techniques are theoretically possible and certainly very dramatic so in the theatre we shall use them. We'll go over all of them in this section. The differences between the same steps in the Wide Stance are small but significant.

Thwarts -

Thwart Left

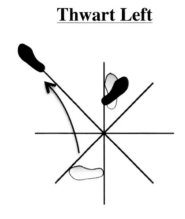

Thwart Right

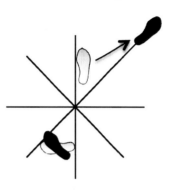

The right foot on the Thwart Right now must traverse to get to the Forward 45° right line. In both Thwarts, the posting foot should pivot as it is unloaded so as to lunge properly.

Fig. 15: **Fabris**- Italy - 1606

Thwart to the 90 Left

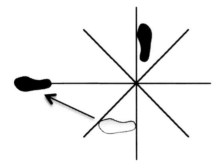

Thwart to the 90 Right

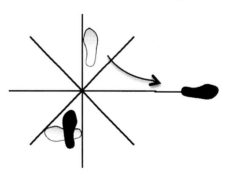

We see again that the major change from the Wide Stance is that the feet must traverse farther with each step in order to get to the same 90° line. Be careful not to step too deeply and go to the plain of the posting foot.

Be sure to pivot the back foot.

Crosses

Cross Left

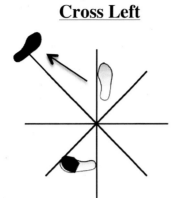

Cross Right

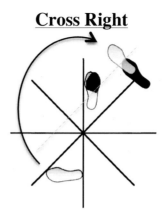

The Cross Right is a very difficult move from a narrow RFF stance and probably will not be used. We can cheat and step on a 45° forward line coming out of the right foot, which is a more reasonable step. One disadvantage of any Cross Right using a weapon designed exclusively for a Narrow Stance, however, is that this move brings the upper body facing the partner, which would be contrary to the philosophy of these weapons. **The Cross Left, on the other hand, is an effective move and will be used much.** You will notice that, in comparison to the Wide Stance, the feet in the this stance are almost crossed anyway, so the Cross Left remains an efficient move – more so than the same move from a wider stance.

Slips

Slip Left

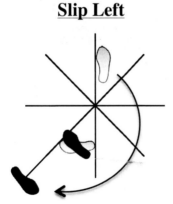

Slip Right

The Slip Left must compass all the way around the left foot and is a large if not exciting move. The Slip Right, on the other hand, is actually smaller and more efficient than the same step from a Wide Stance.

Fig 16: **Angelo** - England - 1763

See the side bar on page 48 for a more detailed look at this particular historical move.

Slip to the 90 Right	Slip to the For. 45 Right
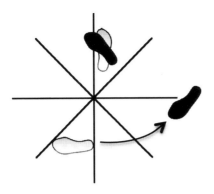	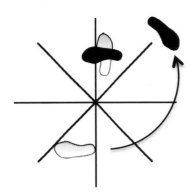

These two moves to the right are performed just as in a Wide Stance. Be sure to compass around (move the foot circularly) and hit the lines with accuracy. The posted foot must change its angle to accommodate the size of these steps.

Fig 17: **Giganti** - Italy – 1606

Fig 18: **Thibaust** - Spain – 1628

In the 18th century school of Smallsword, there is a variant to these two moves called **Demi-Volte** and **Volte**. These were very well known and standard terms at the time and are still used today by some to describe these similar moves. Therefore, we can get progressively more specific when talking about these steps. From the general term **Traverse** to the more specific - **Slip**, to the very specific - **Demi-Volte**; which is a type of Slip to the 90 Right, or a **Volte**; which is similar to a Slip to the Forward 45 Right.

See the next chapter for descriptions of these specific steps.

The Big Picture

What we have done in this section is describe, in specific terms, the performance and proportion of off line steps. Nothing has changed, really, from earlier sections except that we have increased our vocabulary of moves available to us to perform; the process remains the same.

You need to continually remind yourself of the concept of the "neutrality" of each step while performing them. Perform them as they are presented in this section and the following drills as foundational drilling. The long-term goal is to perform any and all steps variable in size, depth and proportion given the circumstance of the moment. With that said, however, try not to get ahead of yourself; it is very important to be specific while training through this section. Like in earlier sections, the goal is to establish landmarks that will allow you to realize when you are stepping on the correct angle, or off that angle – or in proportion or out of proportion.

Drills

1. Stand over your Star and perform all the steps: Concentrate upon hitting the lines correctly, then recovering back to your starting position. Start by looking down to ensure you are not training bad habits, then try not to look until after you perform the step.
   a. Go around the Star performing all the Posted Thwarts, then Crosses, then Slips.
   b. Starting with the Forward 45 line, perform all the steps on that line, then the 90 Right line, Back 45 line, etc.
2. Make sure, after each step, that you check the depth of you step. Review the dotted lines on the diagrams in this section to make sure. With the Crosses and Slips, the standard step is defined by just stepping past the line of your posted foot. Pull the posted foot back along the dotted line to your moving foot to find this out.

COMMON MISTAKES

Not stepping directly upon the line.

Stepping too deeply along the line.

On a Cross – not pointing the moving foot toward the imaginary partner.

Leaning back in the step, especially in the Slip.

Allowing the hips and posted foot to be unspecific.

Not ending steps other than a posted Thwart in a 50/50 weight distribution.

Fig. 19: **Agrippa** - Italy - 1568

Chapter II: Period Specific & Combination Steps

This chapter will concentrate on steps that are more complex to the student because they are either subtle variations of steps we already know, or simply more challenging on a mechanical level because two steps are connected together.

In the first chapter, the focus was on creating a basic, consistent vocabulary and series of physical parameters in order for the student to learn a simple lexicon of definitions with the only variance being the width of the stance. This simplistic, generalized application is designed to allow the student specific parameters with which to drill and critique themselves. On this basic level, one may perform with any weapon and any time period and have a foundational understanding of what they are doing and why - supporting an attack, parrying and avoiding with firm footwork both linear and off-line.

In this Chapter, we will explore steps that, if introduced to the beginner, has the potential of confusing them by giving contradictory, or historically specific information. By giving too many angles on a compass, or too many positions to memorize with various shades of gray to learn, the beginning student will simply generalize all the information. So, if the student has mastered the basics then they are ready for this chapter.

A. Volte and Demi-Volte

Both the Volte and Demi-Volte are specific to the **Narrow Stance** of Smallsword which had a certain line and posture. Although they are **Slips**, they are more linear, with the legs straighter and the overall look being graceful and upright which is in contrast to the earlier Italian Rapier play, which could be described as "down and dirty." Because of these differences, certain changes happen in the execution of the steps.

Demi-Volte

> **DEFINITION**
>
> **Demi – Volte:** A method of effacing the target by swinging the rear leg backward and sideways, so that the trunk is brought 90 degrees in relation to the attack.

A Demi-Volte, or half a Volte, is a **Slip to the 90 Right**, but the feet, in this step, are much closer together and the legs straighter. The angle reference line comes out of the center of the posted foot, but you can see, coincidentally, that the left foot is also on the forward 45 Right. The Slipping foot moves in a straight line instead of a circle as in a Slip.

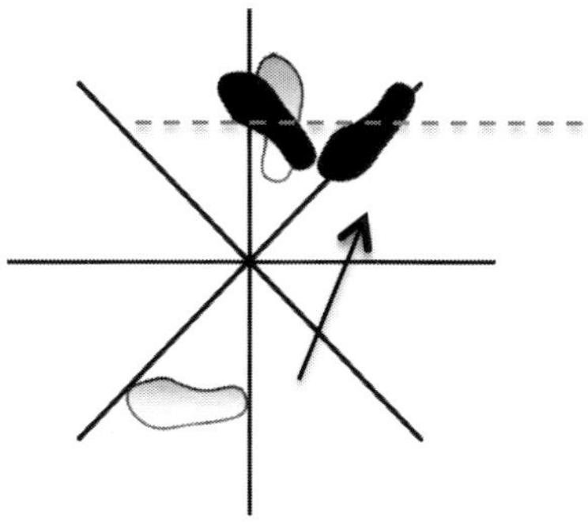

Fig. 20: **Angelo** – England - 1765

Volte

> **DEFINITION**
>
> **Volte:** A method of effacing the target by swinging the rear leg backwards and sideways, so that the trunk is brought 180 degrees in relation to the attack.

The Volte is a Slip to the Forward 45, but, again, is performed much tighter than a regular Slip because of the overall posture of the move. We therefore Slip on a 45 Degree line coming out of the posted foot so that the two feet are closer together. Instead of a circular step, you perform it in a slightly angled straight line.

Fig. 21: **Angelo** – England - 1765

So, if you compare the relative size and dynamics of the Demi-Volte and Volte in Figures 20 and 21 to the Slip to the Forward 45 as illustrated by Capo Fero below, you can see the efficiency of the two former moves as opposed to the largeness of a similar move with a heavier weapon. Look at the line of the body, its posture and where the center of gravity lies.

Fig. 22: **Capo Fero** - Italy – 1610

B. The Half-Passe

The 16th century fight masters generally believed you must clear the line of attack free of obstacles before moving forward. In fact, they thought a Full Passe Forward suicidal if performed on-line. Until the Advance, Retreat and Lunge were developed, the only option was a hop forward or a Passe, and masters recommended stepping forward off-line, or on a Half-Passe, as being much safer. The Half-Passe forward is a "cheating step" that brings the rear foot, in a one-foot forward stance, up to the forward foot before completing the step. There is a slight pause between the 1st and the 2nd half, and this "beat" in the rhythm can be used to clear the way for an attack while moving forward in a controlled manner.

The action of bringing the rear foot up to the forward foot was a good compromise between moving in close enough for a clearing action, while not accidentally stepping into a counter attack or time thrust. The Half-Passe allowed the attacker to move his body forward without over committing the weight of the body in any direction and so was a viable 1st move for any attack, both linear and off-line. In both the Thwart and Cross, performed with the Half-Passe, you will discover that the steps, in fact, go forward even if they are off-line, so distance was closed but traveled around the Gaurdias instead of through them.

A Half-Passe back is performed by removing the forward foot back to the rear foot. This can be an effective avoidance without performing a full Passe Back.

What this provides, for our use in **Stage Combat**, is another way to approach all of the steps we have already learned, both linear and off-line. It can add another beat in the rhythm of the fight, give you another choice of dynamic, and will change the nature of each step.

The Half Passe is indigenous to early Rapier so the diagrams in this section will focus on the Wide Stance, but understand that these moves can be performed from a Narrow Stance especially if you are performing, say, a Rapier fight from the early to middle 17th century where you have chosen to narrow up your stance. If, however, you are performing a Smallsword fight from the 1690s and later, these moves and their style might work against you; they may confuse the very specific style of Smallsword fighting, creating the illusion of the fighter having bad form. Theatrically this could be a choice, but other choices to express bad form may be more appropriate. A Half-Passe is a controlled and proportioned move, done for a very specific tactical reason.

Fig 23: **Agrippa** - Italy – 1568

1. Half Passe Forward

> **DEFINITION**
>
> **Half Passe Forward:** The action of bringing the back foot up to the front foot in preparation to take a 2nd Step. For the 2nd half, you can either:
> 1. Continue   2. Change   3. Return

The First Half

This **Transitional** step is universal, and from where the name "Half-Passe" comes. It is performed the same way with every forward step following.

Starting with a Wide RFF stance, bring the rear foot to the forward foot, following the diagonal line on which both feet are placed.

Notes:
1. The moving foot ends with only the ball of the foot on the ground and the arch of that foot firmly against the posted foot.
2. The symbol of a foot with the heel off the floor is ● .

The Second Half

First we look at these steps in linear terms.

The completion of the step can be done one of three ways:

Continue - Change - Return

a. Continue - The foot that moved simply **continues** on for a full Passe Forward.

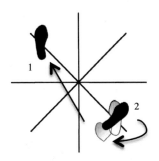

Notes:
1. After the moving foot has gone to the posted foot, it now continues forward out to a standard En Garde (In this case with the LFF).
2. If the step stops here, the posting foot must pivot to finish the En Garde - just like a Passe Forward.
3. The Star has moved forward with the step.

Put the 1st half and a **Continue** together and it looks like this. →

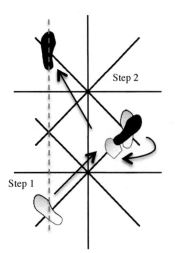

Notes:
1. Notice how the action describes a triangle.
2. There should be a slight pause between step #1 and 2.

b. Change - After the 1st half is completed, the feet change and the opposite foot completes the step.

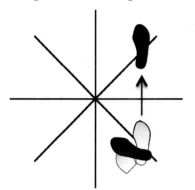

Notes:
1. The foot has gone to the posting foot and now they change: The Right foot kicks out to maintain, in this case, a RFF stance.
2. This step **maintains** the stance, and as such may be considered a viable alternative to the Advance.

Put the 1st. half and a Change together and it looks like this:
1. Half Passe Forward
2. Change Step

Notes:
This move will offset the body to one side: towards the right in a wide RFF stance and will end with you in a Narrow Stance. If you need to adjust back to the line of engagement for **drilling**, do this:

Adjust out with the left foot. (step #3)

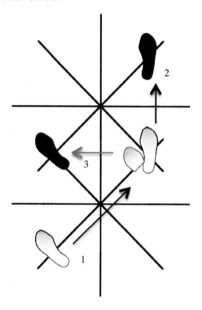

c. Return - The rear foot returns to the original En Garde position.

Notes:
1. This simple move places the left foot back upon the back 45 left line of the Star.
2. This can be a good placement exercise for the back foot – making sure it is placed directly on the back 45 line and at a correct angle and depth.
3. Be sure to end with a 50/50 weight distribution.

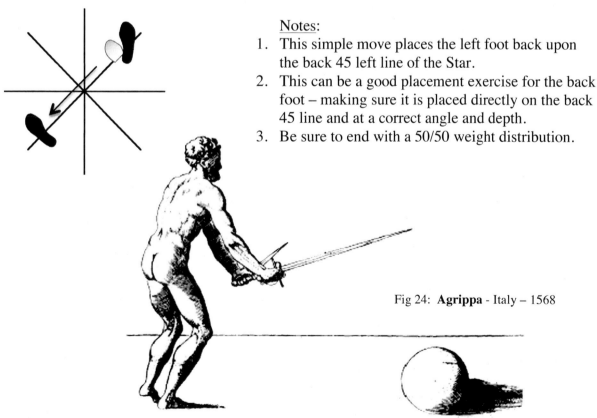

Fig 24: **Agrippa** - Italy – 1568

Off - Line Steps with a Half-Passe Forward

The 1st. step of the Half-Passe will always remain the same, in either a RFF or a LFF stance. Once the performer is in this "cat stance" so to speak, he/she can go anywhere they choose on the Star.

In specific terms, we will be performing Thwarts, Crosses and Slips. But look to see in general terms which of these steps are **Continues** or **Changes**.

Thwarts

Half-Passe Forward Thwart Left   Half-Passe Forward Thwart Right

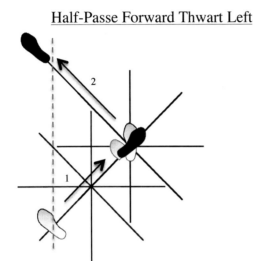 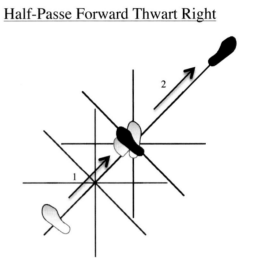

The **Half-Passe Thwart Right** is a <u>Change</u> step while the **Half-Passe Thwart Left** is a <u>Continue</u> step. Notice on the Thwart Left, that the new line to step upon emanates from **between** the feet after step number one.

Thwarts on all Angles from a Half Pass Forward

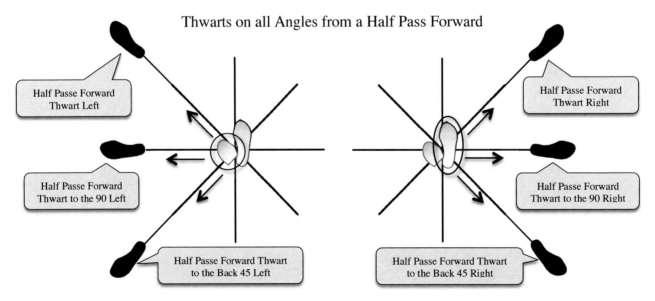

Remember to perform the Thwart as a **Standard Lunge** – we will learn about different size steps in a later chapter.

- 53 -

Crosses

<u>Half-Passe Forward Cross Left</u>　　　　　<u>Half-Passe Forward Cross Right</u>

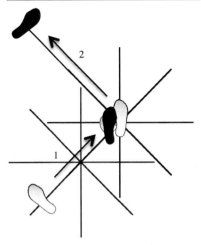
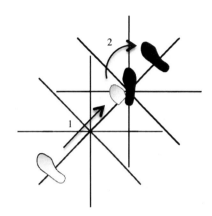

The Half-Passe Cross Right is a <u>Continue</u> step while the Half-Passe Cross Left is a <u>Change</u> Step. The Posted foot on either Cross may lift the heel as in a standard Cross.

Crosses on all Angles from a Half Pass Forward

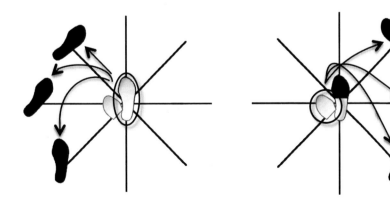

Slips

Half-Passe Forward Slip Left
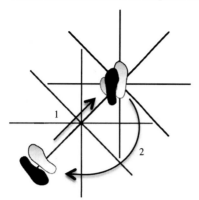

Half-Passe Forward Slip Right
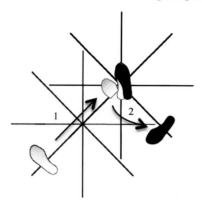

This move is good for an initial attack forward then a change of direction to avoid a counter thrust or attack.

names through al this work, they maie the better be vnderstood.

It is to be knowen that the feete moue either streightly, either circulerly: If streitly, then either forwardes or backwards: but when they moue directly forwards, they frame either a halfe or a whol pace. By whole pace is vnderstood, when the foot is carried from behind forwards, kepinge stedfast the forefoot. And this pace is sometimes made streight, sometimes crooked. By streight is meant when it is done in the streit line, but this doth sel-

B. Half-Passe Back

DEFINITION

Half Passe Back: The action of bringing the forward foot back to the rear foot in preparation to take a 2nd step. Can be used as a <u>Reassemblement</u>.
For the 2nd half, you can either: 1. <u>Continue</u>   2. <u>Change</u>   3. <u>Return</u>

The forward foot draws back to the rear foot - From there you can either **Continue** for a Full Passe Back, **Change** in order to maintain your RFF, or **Return** to your original stance.

Fig. 25: **Alfieri** - Italy – 1640

Slips

Half Passe Back Slip Left   Half Passe Back Slip Right

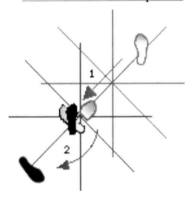   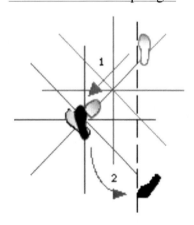

While the step to the left continues on the same back 45 line, the Slip Right back 45 line emanates from the back foot. Make sure you displace your body just as in a standard Slip Right. In other words, step deep enough on that line so that you still have effaced the body.

C. The Hop

> **DEFINITION**
>
> **Hop:** An explosive movement forward by kicking the forward foot forward, while keeping the back foot underneath the body with a hop. Both feet land simultaneously.

This linear step, sometimes called a "jump", is an explosive movement forward similar to the advance, but performed in one count, as opposed to the Advance which is performed in two counts: step forward and recover. This Hop, is performed by simultaneously pushing with the back leg as you kick forward with the lead leg, and, before landing either foot, the back leg hops forward to stay underneath the performers center of gravity. The forward foot pulls back to the ground so that it lands on the floor at the exact moment the back foot lands on the hop.

Some schools of fence consider this single move a Ballestra, but just as many schools consider this only the first move of a two part step called the Ballestra. I concur with the former. The "hop", however, can be a nice aggressive choice of step all by itself.

Start in a Narrow Stance, and raise your forward foot. While keeping the foot raised, begin to lightly kick the foot out and let the momentum carry you forward. Before you fall forward, skip you posted leg back under your center of gravity to maintain your balance. Practice this until you can finish the move in balance and immediately go on to another hop.

Next, use the timing you developed in the first exercise, to coordinate your front foot to reverse direction after the initial kick, and return to the floor at the same time the back foot lands on the hop

Notes:
1. Keep all momentum going forward, not upwards.
2. When you land, be sure to maintain your En Garde stance, do not bring the feet together.

D. Combination Steps

Linear

All of these linear combination steps were developed later in the sword's history and are more commonly used with a Narrow Stance. All but the Fléche are combinations involving the Lunge and if performed in the Narrow Stance, no adjustments will be needed. The Narrow Stance will be shown here, if performing these steps from a Wide Stance, simply stay on the "rails" as explained in Chapter I. Or, you may narrow your stance at the beginning of the step and adjust back out (if necessary in the choreography) at the end.

Reprise, Remise and Redoublement

> **DEFINITION**
>
> **Reprise:** A combination of a Recovery Forward and a Lunge. There are two counts in this action, 1. Recover, 2. Lunge. Also known as Reprise to the Fore.

These moves were developed to reach an opponent who continuously retreats out of distance whenever you lunge. What you decide to do with your sword will determine whether you are performing a Reprise, Remise or Redoublement.

All 3 types of steps are actually started from a Lunge (move #1). After move #1, Step #2 is a simple Recovery Forward. Step #3 is another Lunge.

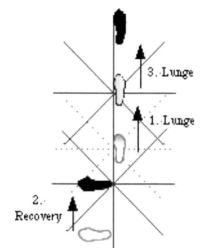

Notes:
1. On step #2, the Forward Recovery, make sure you stay low. Do not straighten your legs at that moment - this transition into the 2nd. Lunge should be smooth and solely in the direction of the attack - not up and down.
2. If performing a **Reprise**, the Recovery Forward momentarily puts you back into an En Garde.
3. If performing a **Remise**, the Sword arm must stay extended throughout the technique: No piston thrusts. The left hand, however, may be articulated.
4. To practice a **Redoublement**, recover your arm on the forward recovery and either thrust or cut again.

Pattinando

> **DEFINITION**
>
> **Pattinando:** A combination of an Advance and a Lunge. There are 2 counts in this action: 1. Advance, 2. Lunge. Also known as... Advance-Lunge.

Like the Reprise, the Pattinando was developed to reach an opponent who continuously retreats out of distance whenever you lunge. Instead of reactionary, like the Reprise, which after missing the target, reacts to this by recovering and lunging again, the Pattinando is tactical in that the plan is to move forward very aggressively from the beginning. The dynamic of this step is one of exploding through the advance into the lunge.

Notes:
1. Be sure that the back foot on the Advance recovers to an En Garde before the Lunge; not up to the forward foot.
2. Perform a Standard size lunge - it will be easy to over extend the lunge because of the extra energy this moves creates.
3. Extend the sword arm before the first advance, and keep it extended during the remainder of the move.

Ballestra

> **DEFINITION**
>
> **Ballestra:** A combination of a Hop forward and Lunge. There are 2 counts in this action: 1. Hop, 2. Lunge. Also known as a Hop-Lunge or Jump-Lunge.

Meaning "Ballistic" the Ballestra is very similar to the Pattinando as being an explosion into a preliminary move before going into a lunge. This move is also intended to reach an opponent on the lunge who continuously moves out of distance. The first step on this move is the **Hop** and which you perform before driving into a lunge.

Notes:
1. Maintain your En Garde through the hop - when both feet land, they should be in Proportion.
2. Perform a Standard size lunge - it will be easy to over extend the lunge because of the extra energy this moves creates.
3. Extend the sword arm before the Hop, and keep it extended during the remainder of the move.

Fléche

> **DEFINITION**
>
> **Fléche:** Literally translated as "Arrow". An attack made by leaping or jumping forward with your rear foot crossing past your front foot.

The Fléche is a running attack. This is a gigantic move but can be effective as a do or die tactic or a competitive fencing move against someone who keeps out of distance.

As you extend your arm, shift your weight to your forward foot, as you continue to drive through with your right and just before you loose your balance, cross over with your left foot which begins a short run towards the opponent.

Notes:
1. Extend your arm before moving
2. Be sure to attempt this only with a qualified instructor present.

Off Line

At this point we can get creative with our off-line steps and combine steps together in all sorts of ways. Just as a Pattinando is a combination of two linear steps: an Advance and a Lunge. These combination steps are performed in similar ways. Here are a few examples of combining steps.

Wide stance, Right foot forward

Combination #1 - Cross, Thwart.

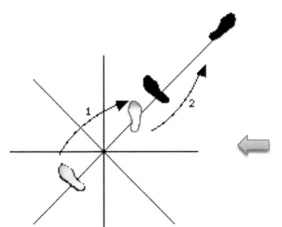

Here the concept of the Thwarts and Crosses simply being 2 parts of a double Passe on a forward 45 degree line reveals itself. Simply stay on the 45-degree line.

These Passes will be like the Crossovers and Passes you have done in the Narrow Stance because you are stepping on a single line as opposed to a pair of parallel rails in the Wide Stance.

Combination #2 - Thwart Right, Slip Right

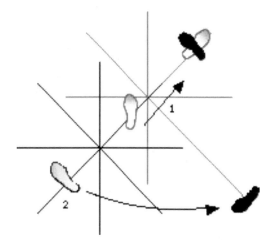

This is a good "in and out" move, or an attack to the Right (inside line or a Mandiritti) followed by an avoidance. Be sure to pivot the posted foot.

Combination #2A
Thwart Left, Slip Left

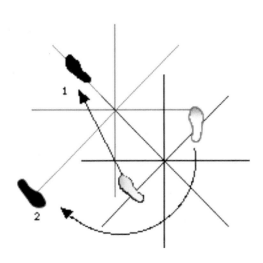

Here, the 1st. Thwart has more momentum from a RFF stance and can carry you very effectively off line.

In both # 2 and 2A, you can begin to play with the momentum of the steps so that the nature of the combination will be more like the Pattinando so that the Thwart will send you fluidly into the Slip.

E. The Sitting Thwart

This is a variation of the Thwart that we have already learned. On the basic level, we drilled the Thwart as a lunge that is physically identical to a forward lunge except for the line it is performed upon, and any adjustments needed to perform it safely (things like adjusting the posted foot). Or, as an "advancing" Thwart where the advance is performed on a specific line. In both steps, the Thwart faces the line and not the partner.

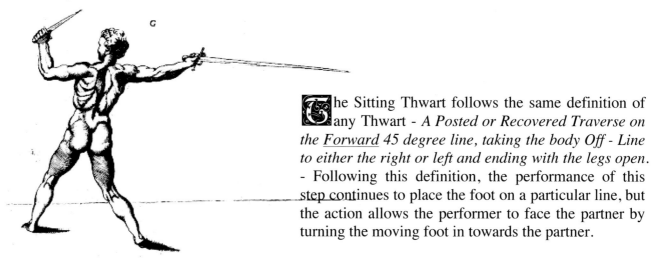

The Sitting Thwart follows the same definition of any Thwart - *A Posted or Recovered Traverse on the <u>Forward</u> 45 degree line, taking the body Off - Line to either the right or left and ending with the legs open.* - Following this definition, the performance of this step continues to place the foot on a particular line, but the action allows the performer to face the partner by turning the moving foot in towards the partner.

Sitting Thwart Right

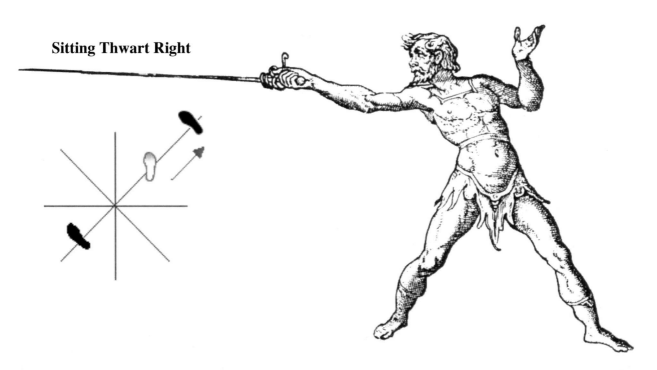

Perform this Thwart by stepping on the forward 45 line, but the lunging foot ends up parallel to the posted foot, or perpendicular to the forward 45 line. Be careful to watch your knee placement while performing this move.

Sitting Thwart to the 90 Right

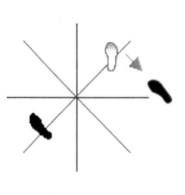

A sitting Thwart to the 90 involves more of a side-stepping action and involves the knee of the moving leg to turn in and sink. This action is very similar to a Cross punch that, in order to allow the knee to work in line with the energy, sinks down on the execution.

This step can be performed either posted or recovered, but, like the standard Thwart, the style of late 16th century/early 17th century works better on a single time step.

Figure 33 - Capo Fero 1610, Figures. 34 & 35: Agrippa - Italy – 1568

Chapter III: Advanced Concepts and Drills

A. Size of the Steps and Keeping Distance

As you are learning these steps, drilling and making your form consistent, another factor will come into play: size. It is not enough to simply know what angle or line upon which to place your foot, you must know how deeply to step along that line. Every variation of size will have a direct influence on the distance between you and your partner. If you step too deeply at the wrong time, you could create an unsafe moment. This section will address how to find, recognize and drill your personal standard step and then how to adjust your steps (and therefore distance) to any situation.

We want our steps to be accurate and consistent. When we work with a partner, we want to be in complete control; whether you are maintaining fencing measure or closing distance for infighting, your distance should be a conscious choice, not a vague approximation of what the choreography says. If your partner is the exact physical size as you, it is easy maintaining your distance as long as you know the size of your own step and are consistent. This is rarely the case, however, and we end up working with someone taller or shorter which means you must change the size of your step to adjust to the situation. Also, the world is not perfect, so mistakes happen and the perfect distance you and your partner were maintaining beautifully all of a sudden dissolves and you are left with a situation witch you must fix by adjusting the size of your step. Knowing your standard step *cold* will allow you to adjust those steps larger or smaller with confidence.

Once we are in control of our steps, distance and form, we still have one last thing to consider. After the choreography has been memorized, our job as actors is to create a dynamic of stepping towards or away from an attack and/or throwing the body off line in a desperate attempt to avoid a fatal attack. So, we must be able to eventually show those desperate dynamics while, at the same time, remain in a relaxed and balanced state. Understanding the parameters and form of your steps will inform you on; how deep you are stepping, how the chosen size effects the step, how it effects distance, and understanding this process of discovery will allow you to layer on these desperate dynamics safely and consistently as you choose the size of **each step** to reflect the dramatic choice of that moment.

Fig. 20: **Danet** - French – 1787

At this point, we will not drill each step within one inch variations, but we can define and drill the two outer landmarks and the step that is in the middle. To that end we will learn three different size steps in this section:

        1. Shallow   2. Standard   3. Deep

> **DEFINITION**
>
> **Standard Step:** a). The established middle landmark for any step within the structure of three sizes of steps: Shallow, Standard and Deep.
> b). The neutral execution of any step.

We have already begun to define **Standard** Passes, Advance/Retreats and Lunges earlier in this book. We will begin by breaking the **Lunge** down into three steps because it is the simplest step to define.

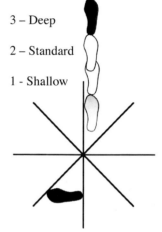

Linear Steps
The Lunge – Narrow Stance

The **Shallow Lunge** can be a half-hearted attack, or an attack that needs a little more than a lean-in, or as an adjusted lunge when you are too close to the target.

    The length of the shallow lunge is **one foot**.

To find this Lunge, perform an Advance with the forward foot while **leaving the rear foot posted**. This is explained earlier in detail on page 21.

> *Tip: placing a piece of tape on the floor at the tip of your lead foot can give you a target.*

> **From page 24….**
> For the first part of the Advance, look down at your forward foot, and in one swift move, replace the tips of your toes with your heel. This means you must pivot your foot upward, bringing your toes up and placing your heel on the floor.

Your **Standard Lunge** is a more committed Lunge and your goal while drilling to establish consistent form. This "middle step" is the basis in which you will adjust your step larger or smaller for either the moment, the size of your partner, or eventually the mistakes of you and your partner.

    To find this Lunge, while in a Shallow Lunge:

> **From page 27…**
> Note where the ball of your right foot is on the floor, mark it, and advance the front foot a second time so that the heel is at that spot.
> **The depth of your Lunge is now 1¾-foot length.**

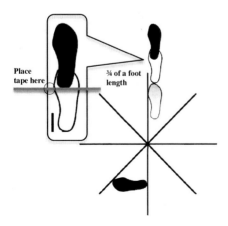

> **More from 27…**
> **NOTE:** Two full foot lengths may be appropriate for those who have fencing training or martial arts or whatever has helped them develop strong legs. A beginner will be better off with a Standard Lunge of only 1¾-foot length. Studying with a competent teacher will insure both safety and good form. Whatever size you choose; make it consistent.
> A qualified teacher should assist

The **Deep Lunge** is a finito move that might end the fight, or an adjusted Lunge if you are too far away from the target. Because this highly dramatic move is deeply extended, putting a strain on the front knee and hamstrings, we may train it to develop strength, but perform it only occasionally in choreography. You must be careful and not get into the habit of "working too hard" on your Standard Lunge and save the Deep Lunge and your knees for when you need it. The size of this Lunge is **2 ¾-foot lengths**.

> To find this Lunge, while in your Standard Lunge, mark the tip of your forward foot and once again place your heel on that mark.

Wide Stance

From page 28:

> ### Wide Stance
>
> In the Wide Stance, valuable leg length is lost when maintaining the "rails". So, we narrow our feet slightly – the 1st step narrows the stance by ½ foot width. The second step (1 ¾ deep) is also narrowed by ½ a foot width. The final position of the front foot is closer to the forward 90 line, but not next to the line as in the Narrow Stance.
>
> *Be especially aware of the hips and forward knee in this Lunge. A tendency will be to turn the hips toward the side 90 and allow the forward knee to fold inward (Hip Relationship; section A).
>
>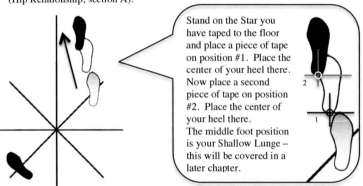
>
> Stand on the Star you have taped to the floor and place a piece of tape on position #1. Place the center of your heel there. Now place a second piece of tape on position #2. Place the center of your heel there.
> The middle foot position is your Shallow Lunge – this will be covered in a later chapter.

Recalling how we found the **Standard Lunge** on page 24, continue in the same way by placing a piece of tape at the front and side of your Standard right foot Lunge. Then place the center of your heel on the tape to find your **Deep Lunge**.

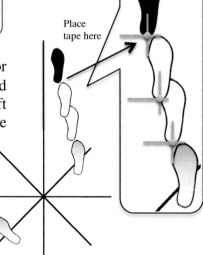

In the Wide Stance, Lunges may be performed with either the left or right foot. You may find yourself in a defensive LFF stance and asked to Lunge with the left foot, or you might be asked to perform a left Lunge while in a RFF stance, which means you must learn to Passe Forward and Lunge in one motion. This will be covered later.

The size of all these Lunges, of course, is relative to the performer. Each person will have different size feet, longer legs or the ability to Lunge deeper. It is important to establish your sizes, and then be consistent. If your students train hard and master this system, they will develop a sense of self-adjustment while performing the Lunge, and will then be able to adjust their step when needed.

From page 28

A	D

Remember your form!
For both Narrow and Wide Stances, no matter what size:

A. The forward foot should travel and end completely straight and parallel to the forward 90 line. Be careful not to allow the foot to "sickle" inward.
B. The forward lower leg is perpendicular to the ankle, so that the knee is bent and over the ankle, **not past the toes**. To check this, look down over your knee **without leaning forward** and you should just see the outline of your foot around the knee.
C. The back leg is straightened – *completely,* but not hyperextended.
D. The back foot is firmly on the ground. Be sure not to allow the foot to roll over to its side. This foot is your "anchor" as it grounds your movement.
E. The upper body is straight up and down without any leaning forward.
F. Just as in the Advance, the **hips** and **shoulders** maintain their angle; unchanged from your En Garde. The combination of the hips tuning toward the side 90 and the foot sickling inward will put the forward knee in danger.

More Lunge Variables while Extending the Arm

When we extend our Sword before the Lunge, there are more variables that effect distance. These variables are connected with and added to the ones above.

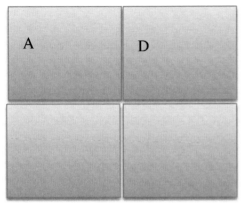

1. Turning (rotating) the upper body toward or away from the forward 90 line.

   Side by side pict of body rotating

2. While extending, rolling (hyperextending) the right shoulder forward.

   Side by side pict of Shoulder hyperextending

3. Leaning the upper body forward.

4. Not fully extending the sword arm.

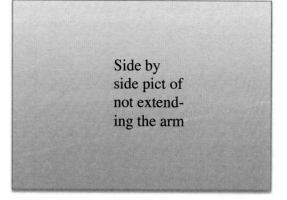

What all these variables do is move the point of the weapon either inside safe distance or outside believable distance while performing **the exact same Lunge with the feet**. So, first we must be patient and learn the most consistent Lunge without any of the above variables and consider this a mastery of good form.

The upcoming drills will help.

Fig. 21: **Sir William Hope** – Scotland - 1710

Lunging on a Cutting Attack

Lunging on a cutting attack is more advanced because you do not have the "early warning device" of the thrust to help you decide the size of you Lunge. Learn and master the thrusting attack **first** and the awareness you develop will serve you for the cutting attack.

The Big Picture

Most of us who have been preforming for many years develop the awareness we are focusing on here. We develop an instinct that allows us to maintain the dynamic of the moment while making safety adjustments in real – time. These instincts reflect training over the years but even a seasoned performer or teacher may not be able to quickly teach these concepts that they can perform, but can't really articulate to a student.

The reason we began learning this concept with the Lunge is because, as a fully committed thrusting or cutting attack, it is the last chance to **adjust** your distance before completing that attack. The ideal circumstance is that we always perform our steps and move in perfect distance to our partner. When it is time to Lunge, the ideal is to perform the size you chose in rehearsal – and what the choreography says. This allows you to fully commit to the Lunge without any hesitation or deceleration. This, however, does not always happen and suddenly, when it comes time to Lunge, you find yourself either too close or far away. Drilling your **Standard**, **Shallow** and **Deep** Lunges will give you definite landmarks that your muscle memory can recreate, can reach for, and yet allow you to spontaneously adjust with accuracy.

TIME

Every action, every movement takes **Time** to perform. From the pointing of a finger to an extension of the arm takes a moment of time – time we can use for our advantage in the execution of technique, and it is this clarity or preciseness that can communicate – to both your partner and the audience.

Fig. 22: **Rosaroll** and **Gresetti** – Italy - 1803

Some moves take more Time, some less. If both the start and ending positions are specific, and you can consistently perform the action the same way, you can start to Time out that action. For example, the extension of the sword arm before the Lunge takes a specific amount of Time to perform. With a good En Garde, the time it takes to extend is short, but if your sword is out of En Garde – say after a parry – it takes longer to get to the same extension. To make it specific to the footwork; if your feet are in a specific Stance, and you are consistent with performing a specific Lunge, then the Time will be consistent as well.

So, once you understand kinesthetically the size of these three Lunges, and can consistently perform them, you begin to understand that each one takes a certain amount of **Time** to perform with the Shallow Lunge taking less Time and each progressively larger Lunge taking more.

Now, with this new awareness (that will be drilled in the next section) you can begin to adjust the size of your step through knowledge and awareness of **Placement** and **Time** instead of guessing, or panic.

In other words, when attacking with a thrust;
1. In the drill or choreography it is time for you to attack; instantly you gauge the distance between the two of you (the drills on the next page will refine your distance awareness).

2. Extend your arm, which brings the point closer to your partner, giving you more information about how far you need to step. In the **Time** between the finish of the extension and the beginning of the Lunge, you either confirm your distance or modify your choice.
3. You commit and reach for one of the three Lunge sizes you think will deliver the point of your weapon to the appropriate distance.
4. In the midst of performing the Lunge and visually following your point to the target, you confirm if the choice was accurate and complete the step. If there is a need to adjust, the adjustment (hopefully) is minimal, but you now have the **Time** to correct it. If you are too close, all you have to do to stop, or end your Lunge, is top put your forward foot down. If you are little bit short, you reach past it for a few more inches – delivering the point to the correct distance.

You have in fact now adjusted your foot in 1 inch increments.

This also works very well with two people who are of extreme difference in height. The shorter must realize and expect to Lunge slightly deeper than his/her Standard Lunge and the taller must perform a more Shallow Lunge than they do usually.

It is really all about the point, where it is at the end of the attack. The size of the Lunge is secondary.

Drills for Lunges at Different Distances

With a partner, go to a wall that you don't mind placing the point of a sword upon. Your partner will stand by the wall and measure your distance, as well as give you observations and commands.

Stage Combat measure is generally understood to be

Drill #1: Learning Extension Distance.
1. Gently place the tip of your sword onto the wall, straighten your arm and adjust your body to assume a good stance (either wide or narrow – it doesn't matter) with an extended arm. With your partners help, and keeping the point of the sword on the wall, try and eliminate any variables in your stance, torso and arm.
2. Release the point off the wall and assume your En Garde. – Settle into it.
3. Gently extend your arm again – be kind to the wall. Did you shift forward resulting in your arm not fully extending or back resulting in you not reaching the wall? Did you rotate your torso? Your partner may help you with figuring out if there is a variable in your En Garde.
4. While extended, shuffle back in your stance until your point is 7" away from the wall (your partner will measure, and they may use their hand with the thumb and pinky extended – the "call me" gesture.

> **En Garde extention variables:**
> 1. Turning (rotating) the upper body toward or away from the forward 90 line.
> 2. Rolling (hyperextending) the right shoulder forward.
> 3. Leaning the upper body forward.
> 4. Not fully extending the sword arm.
> 5. Rocking your weight either forward or back (weight should be 50/50).

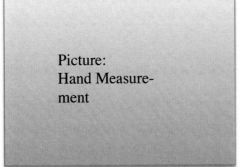
Picture: Hand Measurement

5. Release your extension and assume an En Garde.
6. Extend again and have your partner measure you – did a variable slip in? Do this until all variables are recognized and eliminated.
7. Be sure to take time and see what this distance looks like – the point of your sword can inform you – how far is your body (without relying on lines on the floor as landmarks) – what is the difference between your arm at En Garde and when it is extended? How much distance is used?
8. Now walk away from the wall, then return and try to estimate your extension distance. Remember, your En Garde can inform you about your distance. If your sword tip is out where it should be, the tip being the closest thing to the wall can give you valuable information.
9. Once you have done this a few times – gotten reasonably consistent with your distance and form, walk away and come back to the wall more quickly – make your decision faster – also change up your wall – you can inadvertently work out landmarks with witch you can cheat – lines on the floor, ect.

Drill # 2: Learning your Standard Lunge Distance.
1. Just like the Extension Distance Drill, place your sword point on the wall, extend your arm, shuffle back to good distance, but this time drop into a **standard lunge** by sliding your back foot farther back and straighten the leg. Be sure your form is good – you may have to adjust your form and distance a few times.
2. Recover back into en garde, and then perform you standard lunge again. Watch the point travel toward the wall – your goal is to perform a Standard Lunge without any variables. Your

partner will measure – are you too close? Too far away? If something has changed, locate and eliminate the variable.

3. Continue this exercise at the wall until you can hit your measure consistently. Your partner is there not only to measure your point, but to observe and comment about your form – in a supportive way, let them know if you see anything – be sure to hit a good stance when you recover, and a good, well measured Standard Lunge.
4. Now, walk away. Come back to the wall and try and gauge what your Standard Lunge Distance is. Assume an en garde, the point of the sword will be your "antennae", lunge and your partner will measure. Take your time and adjust, as you need to.
5. Once you are consistent, reduce the time you spend finding your standard lunge distance – be sure to change locations so you don't establish landmarks. Also be sure you are always performing a standard lunge – "take the hit" so to speak – if you are too far or close; do not fix it by making a smaller or larger lunge – that comes later. Learn by allowing yourself to make mistakes.

Drill #3: Learning the Shallow and Deep Distances.
1. Repeat the sequence of exercise 2; first with a shallow lunge then with a deep lunge. Remember, concentrate on judging shallow or deep lunge distance and committing to the size of that particular lunge size and find out how accurate your perception was.

Drill #4: Achieving your distance by adjusting your lunge
1. Walk away from the wall and return to it arbitrarily. Stop, assume an en garde and look at your distance. Knowing your standard lunge, tell your partner what you think you need to do in order to get your point 7" from the wall. If it is slightly bigger or smaller than your standard lunge – say it then perform it. While still in the lunge, gauge 3 things: 1. Are you at good distance? 2. Did you perform what you thought you needed to perform? If not, what did you perform? 3. Did you add in any variables? (try not to)
2. The most important skill we are developing in this drill is to deliver the point to the same spot consistently. Concentrate on this exclusively. If you need to put your foot down sooner than you anticipated while in en garde, so be it – the distance is the important thing now. This also applies to reaching farther than your initial estimate.
3. Have your partner stop you while you are walking toward the wall. Do the same thing; go to en garde, gauge how far you are, announce it then perform it with the flexibility in mind to adjust your decision while performing the lunge.
4. Once you are consistent, walk to the wall; extend while still moving and lunge, stopping your lunge as you achieve your distance with the point. Then run!

Once the student has mastered their lunging form, understands the concept of distance and moving with a partner, they can start to add variables into the lunge such as leaning the body forward, or turning in the shoulder. These then become conscious factors in building the dynamics of either the character or the moment and can be layered on safely. The one factor we do not want to add into a lunge is the overextension of the forward knee. This simply puts too much pressure on the knee and is not, in any situation, worth the danger.

Finding the Size of Other Steps

The Deep Double Passe - Wide Stance Only

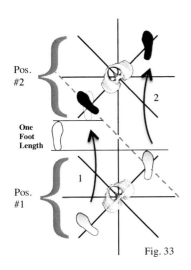

Fig. 33

Starting from a wide En Garde (pos.#1) with your RFF, your feet will be positioned on one diagonal line. In this case, the Forward 45 right, and Back 45 left. To gauge a **Deep Passe Forward**, as mentioned in the previous section, the left foot in step #1 is placed on another 45 line that is in line with the right foot, and running parallel to the Forward 45 left (the dotted line). With every step you take after that, this will be the case. Step #2 brings us back to a RFF En Garde (position # 2). Notice that this is simply an En Garde with both feet on the same line (forward 45 right and back 45 left) as in position #1.

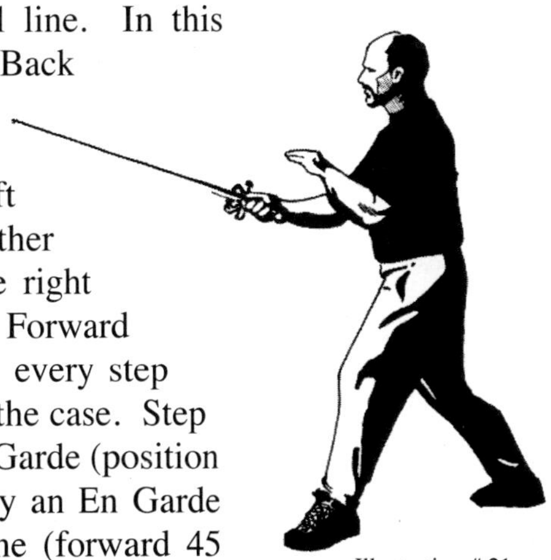

Illustration # 21

Just before the completion of step #1, you have a choice whether to shift the hips and stay in a LFF stance, or **not** shift the hips, and continue on to a Double Passe Forward. If you perform a **Triple Full Passe** in a **wide** stance, the hips would shift on the last step - for it is a change of En Garde in the final move, just as in a Single Passe.

This **Deep Double Passe** represents the large or **deep** aspect of all double passes. In order to reach this rather large step without shifting the hips or falling forward into it, you must lower your center of gravity by bending your posted leg while reaching energetically with the passing leg. This step is an excellent exercise in placement, balance, and establishing your "size landmarks" while training for a size and dynamic that choreography performed at speed may occasionally represent. The smaller **Double Crossover** is a much different step, which we will look at now.

b. Off - Line Steps

Thwarts

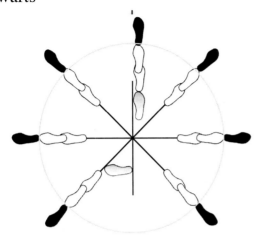

The posted thwart is the same size as your standard lunge (#2). For a shallow thwart you perform a shallow lunge (#1) and for a deep thwart you do a deep lunge. (#3) Even the shallow thwart will displace the body and is an effective move, especially if it is linked with a second move in combination. Simply be sure to follow the appropriate line farther out as you get deeper.

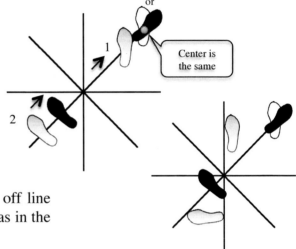

Narrow Stance

The recovered thwart can be done so that the left foot ends either pointing down the line or in it's original orientation moved down the line.
The size is just like in an advance – toe to heel (little toe in this case). If the front foot maintains its alignment, its center is the same as the other.

For the narrow stance, heel to toe would not move you off line enough. So, we use the same final placement of the foot as in the wide stance.

Crosses and slips are a little different. We drill our standard step as the smallest and most efficient step we can perform that will take the body off line and anything larger then is a conscious choice.

Crosses

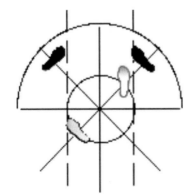

To gauge a standard cross, the crossing foot draws back towards the posting foot. The toes should brush together.

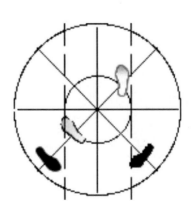

Slips

If you draw the posting foot back, the heel should line up with the toes of the slipping foot.

Drilling the steps with these parameters in place and becoming consistent is mastery of your form and should be considered the foundation of your footwork technique. Any steps that are larger will change your distance and dynamic. When we must step deeper, step on the angled line and not into an obscure area.

Deep Cross

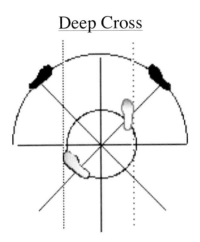

Deep Slip

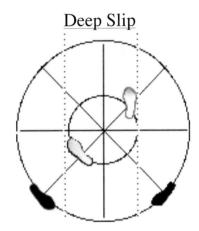

The Standard Cross and Slip are more like Passes in nature where the En Garde is important to maintain. The weight is 50/50 and the hips maintain a relationship facing the partner (see "Hip Relationship). In both deeper steps, the weight is no longer 50/50 but like a Lunge, 60/40. For deep steps, use the size and measurement of your Standard Lunge along the Star as a basis.

Figures 21 + 22: Fabris - Italy – 1606

Figure 16 - Illustration from Domenico Angelo's School of Fencing, showing an off line technique similar to the Slip Right. The House of Angelo; an Italian family who located in London in the mid 17th. Century and became the greatest fencing school in England at the time.

The entire section of the book; illustration and text is reprinted here.

The Parade call'd Prime deriv'd from the Broad-Sword & call'd the St. George Guard against the outside thrust under the wrist call'd Seconde.

PLATE XXI.

In order to parry this outside thrust under the wrist, called seconde, with this prime parade, you must, at the time your adversary thrusts under the wrist, pass your point over his blade, and lower it to the waist, keeping your wrist as high as your mouth, turning your nails downward, your elbow bent, your body kept back as much as possible, and give an abrupt close beat on his blade with your outward edge; as you are then situated, you may, by way of precaution, hang down your left hand, as before mentioned in the Flanconade, and in the same manner, or step out of line.

This opposition is made at the time you parry, and very close, to avoid the adversary's point, if you should want to thrust in a straight line.

To step out of line, must be done at the time you parry the thrust, by carrying your right foot, flat and plumb, about six inches out of line to the right, the left foot also to be carried to the same line about the foot, which will throw you further from the center.

In my opinion, this last motion is preferable to the opposition of the left hand; and as it is practiced in many academies, especially in Italy, I have thought proper to give an explanation of it.

The reason why I prefer this last to the first, is, because the two points being low, and within the swords, it is better to step out of line; and by so doing, you will find the left side of the adversary's body exposed and open.

We see this move in multiple manuals, notably in Saviolo, but let's call this move the "Angelo Slip". The major difference between a regular Slip Right from a Narrow Stance and this move is that there is an adjustment step with the right foot **before** you step off line with you left. It is therefore performed with a 2 beat rhythm and the 2 steps are of equal size.

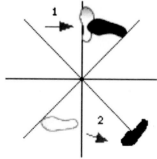

B. Teacher Notes on Drilling

With so many steps, both linear and off-line, as well as names and angles to remember, you might feel intimidated by the apparent complexity of this system; Don't be, it is actually quite simple. Now that we have a basic understanding of how to step on the Star, we can drill the steps using this structure. Understanding the step: the angle and size, is the 1st. step in freeing the body to make minute adjustments in your distance while fighting. Therefore, drill very specifically.

Here are a few tips to help you and your students drill effectively.

I find it best, after taping a Star on the floor and beginning to drill, to separate traveling linear techniques (Advance/Retreat, Passe for/back, Lunge, Pattinando, Ballestra and Fléche) from drill that involves Traverses. The use of the Star with linear techniques is to understand how the feet are positioned and how they move on the "rails", but since the nature of all linear steps are, with the exception of the Lunge, to be constantly leaving that Star, the focus of the drill becomes; can the student return to the Star with their feet in position again - it makes it difficult to keep momentum in drilling when everyone is continually breaking concentration to go back to the Star and reposition their feet. So, after we are comfortable with the linear techniques, drill then in Thwarts, Crosses and Slips.

When first learning or teaching a student, keep it simple. The first idea to get across is that the Thwarts and Crosses are **forward** steps and that the Slip is a **backward** step. <u>These are the simple steps.</u> If no additional information is supplied for that step (with the exception of the direction), it is to be assumed that the step is on the appropriate 45-degree line. For Thwarts and Crosses, therefore, the **Forward 45**, and for Slips, the **Back 45** - anything else is a variation of those steps. Since there are only 3 off line steps in this system, it is easy to learn, but, if you get into explaining all the angles and variations immediately, I find the student gets bogged down with too much information.

I teach the recovered Thwart in the basics because I want to show the consistency of the system; posted/recovered steps on any line and to give options to the teacher and artist. But, I find I personally spend no time teaching these steps outside of the initial introduction.
I do this for a number of reasons;
1. Drilling; it's more efficient to drill all three Traverses and their variations if they are all posted. Recovery to En Garde is simpler – only one foot moves and only one foot recovers – less looking down to the Star, less adjustment time.
2. Style; historically, the timing of Renaissance sword fighting was in **Single Time** (1 count). The Passe, Cross, Slip and posted Thwart are all performed in Single Time and I use them more often in this way. It's true that in later fighting styles the timing evolved to **Double Time** (2 counts) – the Advance/Retreat as well as the Parry/Riposte are examples of this style, but I find I never really use a recovered Thwart probably because of:
3. The Cross and the Thwart represent 2 halves of a Double Passe on the appropriate line chosen, and as such, constitute 2 separate single time actions.
4. Later fighting styles did not use Thwarts except to set up a Slip (see the "Angelo Slip pg. 53).

Fig. 23: Thibaust - Spain – 1628

Proper foot placement on the lines of the Star is important. The diagrams describing the basic steps indicate what alignment the foot should follow. These are basic steps with specific relationships between the foot, knee and hips. Drill with these parameters in place than graduate to different foot - hip - knee relationships (see the following sections).

Once the angles and foot placement are clear, you can drill off-line steps any number of the following ways.
1. Travel around the Star using 1 step, such as the Thwart, covering all the angles, then change to another step and continue again around the Star.
2. Work in terms of angles -- Thwart Right, Cross Right, Slip Right - which are all on 45 degree lines, then change to Thwart to the 90 Right, Cross to the 90 Right, Slip to the 90 Right. - Continuing around the Star.
3. Mix and match -- the posting leg will allow you to drill quickly - simply recover back after each step to an En Garde.

A. Use of the Star

When beginning, the Star is stationary and we work around it hitting all the lines from either a Neutral, RFF, or LFF stance. After there is understanding and consistency with the steps, we can drill without being tied to the Star. The only thing we have to do is recover back to an En Garde after each step, just as if we were performing a Lunge. We then can combine linear, off-line steps and advancing Thwarts in one drill. When this happens, the Star must move with the performer. Therefore, as an example, if you perform a Full Passe Forward, followed by a Cross Left, then the 2nd move, the Cross Left, must be done as if the Star is directly underneath the center of the body *at the time you execute the Cross*.

Thwart Right

Cross Right

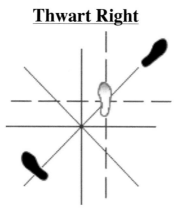

If we step from an En Garde into a Thwart Right the new center of the Star is moved slightly to the Right and forward on the 45 degree line. The Cross ends with the center between the closely spaced feet.

For now, the Star will keep its orientation with the Forward 90 line facing straight ahead without rotating to face any imaginary partner(s).

Fig. 24: Thibaust - Spain – 1628

C. Keeping Distance while Fighting in a Circle

nce you understand the concept of distance and have mastered your form, keeping distance is really very easy: At the basic level, every move your partner performs, you mirror them, and you compensate for size differences or mistakes using your standard step as a basis. For mixed steps, you now know if, for instance, one person Passes and the other Retreats, the person who is Passing should know that they must Passe on a shallower step than their standard while the person Retreating knows that they must Retreat deeper than their standard Retreat. Through the process of rehearsal, the two partners shall discover what they must do for each move.

eeping distance on a circle might look more complicated, but if you use your knowledge of the types, angles, and size of the steps in this system, circular fighting is as easy as matching your partner while performing Linear steps even if the steps themselves are mismatched.

Twin Circles

The first thing to visualize is now, not only your own star, but your partner's. As your partner stands opposite you in Lunging distance, look to see where all four feet are placed. Visually connect the two forward feet with a circle, then do the same for the back feet.

Remember in Chapter 1 when talking about the Advance/Retreat and Passes in the wide stance and visualizing the "rails" so that your feet don't come together? Well these are now the "rails" you use to keep your feet apart while performing the following off-line steps.

The feet will step around the circle, and now for the first time you will not be stepping precisely on the lines of the star, but on the circles; defined by the star.

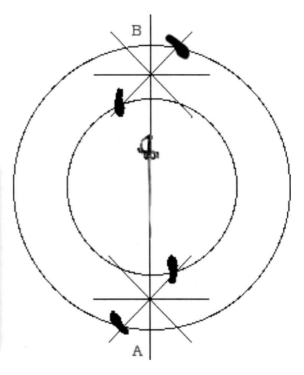

Cool stuff you don't need to know

If you are taping stars to the floor, make each line two feet in length and be sure you are in lunging distance when you create the second star. If your measurements are precise, you will find that the sword you are using in this exercise will fit precisely between the stars. Shades of Thibaust in figure 2! Also look to figure 4 and Morozzo's woodcut to see similar circles.

This first exercise will be a matched - step circular sequence. There are no attacks here, we are traveling around the circles focusing on our distance.

After finding your distance, both A and B perform a cross step. Theoretically, if both of you are of equal height, and your steps are of the same size, you will maintain your distance. Notice here that even though the feet are stepping off line to the left, the position is on the inner circle not precisely on the line of the star.

Next, both of you Thwart to the Left. Again, if you both step on, this time, the outside circle and your steps are the same size you will maintain your distance.

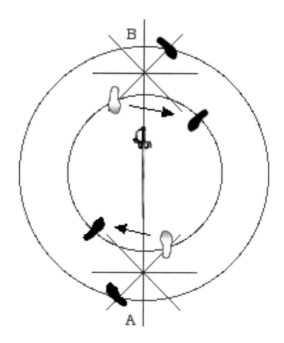

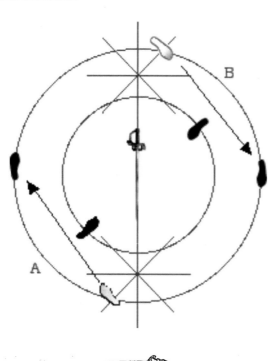

Next, Cross Right again. In most instances, without stepping too deeply or too shallow, it should take you 4 steps to turn 180 degrees. In the 1st Cross, you get 1/4 of the way around the circle, on the Thwarts 1/2 of the way and now we are 3/4 of the way around.

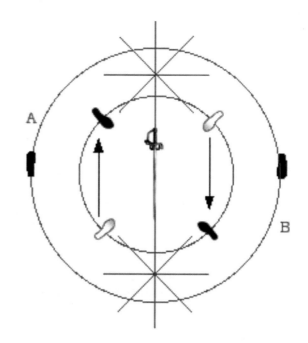

Fig. 36: Aggripa - Italy – 1568

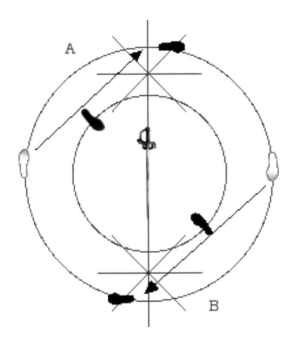

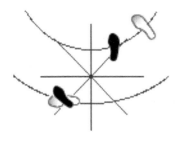

Finally, this last Thwart will bring you onto your partners star. The last thing to do is to make an adjustment step with your right foot in order to get back on the star. Also, pivot to face your partner in a good En Garde.

Problems in keeping distance occur when:

1. The right foot steps inside the inside circle - which decreases distance.
2. The right foot steps onto the outside circle - which increases distance.
3. The left foot steps onto the inside circle - decreasing distance.
4. The left foot steps outside the outside circle - increasing distance.

These adjustments can be a choice when faced with a taller or shorter partner, or when adjusting for dynamics or mistakes. Through these exercises you can recognize the need to adjust very easily.

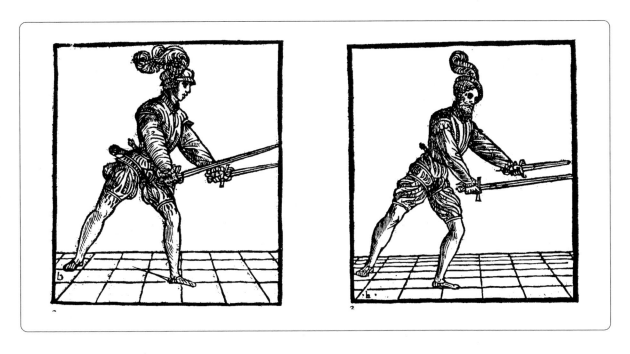

Fig. 37: Morozzo - Italy – 1536

Punto Reversi - Parry 2

This exercise shall take you through a very simple mismatched circular step sequence. It also takes us into the realm of sword fighting and assumes you understand the following sword techniques.

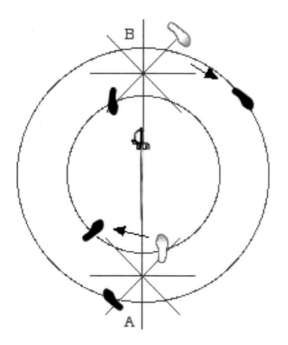

Here, **A** has performed a Cross Left with a Punto Reversi, while **B** has performed a Thwart Left with a parry 2.

Notice here again that both the feet in the Cross Left and the Thwart Left are not stepping on the lines of the Star but on the inside and outside circles. If you are true to the circles, you will find that your distance has been maintained.

In the next step, shown below, B has now progressed from the Thwart to a Cross Left, Punta Reversi, while A now performs a Thwart Left with a Parry 2.

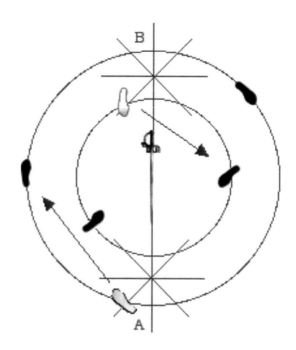

Again, you see that the partners have now traveled one quarter of the way around the circle.

Keep focused on the circles. Remember what creates and diminishes distance.

You can both continue around the circle this way ad infinitum and maintain your distance.

16th and 17th century manual illustrations and how they convey footwork concepts

Grids
Vincentio Saviolo - Italy - 1595

An Italian who taught and published his book: *His Practice* in London, Saviolo shows a grid pattern on the floor.

As does Morrozzo - Italy - 1536

And Fabris - Italy - 1606

Foot patterns.
Sainct Didier - France - 1573

Here we see actual foot marking with a numbered sequence.

Below:
Thibaust - Spain - 1628

Figures 25 & 26 – Angelo's version of the Demi-Volte and Volte

The Half Round or bounding turn of the body calld Demy Volte.

PLATE XXXII

When you are in distance, you must engage the sword in tierce, having the arm flexible, your body well on the left hip, and give your adversary opening sufficient on your outside to engage him to thrust; and at the time he forces your blade, either in tierce or cart over the arm, you must subtiley disengage your point under the mounting of his sword, with your wrist in carte, well opposed, and direct your point to his right breast; at the same time carry your left foot near the right, that the point of your left foot be about two inches behind the right heel, the two feet forming an angle: to complete this position; you ought to keep your knees straight your head erect and in a line with the right shoulder, and the left shoulder well turned out, with a stretched out arm, as in the carte thrust.

It is impossible to complete this volte, or turn of the body, with that vivacity and exactness it requires, without turning the point of the right foot inward, and lifting it up from the ground a little, and turning upon the heel your leg and thigh, as on a pulley, that the body may be more thrown back ina straight line with that of the antagonist, in order to shun the enemy's point; this done, up must recover with your left foot back, and come to a guard according to the rules explained, with the circle parade.

This same demi-volte may be made at the time the adversary advances and forces your blade; the complete executing of this thrust consists in taking just time.

The whole turn calld Volte, on the pass made in Tierce, or in Carte over the Arm.

At the time the adversary disengages within, and thrusts carte, you must raise the wrest to the height of your face, with your nails upward, and with swiftness and agility perform this turn of the body call volte; fixing your point to his right breast, straighten your legs at the time you pass with the left foot behind the right, which distance should be about a foot; your left shoulder should be turned outward, to form a complete side front or profile, to your adversary, your head in a line with your shoulder and arm, to enable you to direct your point forward in that line. The thrust being made, recover your guard with your wrest in tierce, and beat smartly, with the fort of your tierce edge, on the feeble of his sword, raising your wrist and lowering your point.

Glossary of Terms

Terms marked with an * are terms as defined by the Society of American Fight Directors

90 Left - A specific line on an Imaginary Star that consists of 45-degree relationships to the primary North-South and East-West lines. The 90 Left refers then to the line of movement that would be directly west.

90 Right - A specific line on an Imaginary Star that consists of 45-degree relationships to the primary North-South and East-West lines. The 90 Right refers then to the line of movement that would be directly east.

Active Hand - A non sword-bearing arm that is kept in front of the body and used for offense or defense.

Adjustment Step -
1. A small step intended to correct or realign the feet. Usually done very quickly. i.e. Recovery Forward from a Wide Stance.
2. Any step that is not part of a step definition or choreography and is performed for the explicit reason to fix a problem with either distance or angle.

*Advance - [Linear Step] Sometimes referred to as "the fencing step." The leading foot steps forward, followed by the trailing foot.

*Avoidance - A movement intended to "dodge' an attack.

Back 45 - A specific line on an Imaginary Star that consists of 45-degree relationships to the primary North-South and East-West lines. The back 45 refers then to those lines of movement that would be to the South East and South West.

Back 90 - A specific line on an Imaginary Star that consists of 45-degree relationships to the primary North-South and East-West lines. The back 90 refers then to those lines of movement that would be to the South.

*Ballestra - [Linear Step] A combination of a jump forward and a Lunge. There are two counts in this action; one-jump, two-lunge.

Change - See Half Passe

Continue - See Half Passe

*Cross - [Off-Line Step] A Posted, Passing Traverse on the <u>Forward</u> 45-degree line, taking the body Off - Line to either the right or left and ending with the legs crossed.

Crossover, Single - [linear Step] A type of Passe, forward or back, smaller than a Full Passe, that does not change the alignment of the feet, hips or shoulders in it's execution.

Crossover, Double - [linear Step] A type of Double Passe, forward or back, smaller than a Full Passe, that does not change the alignment of the feet, hips or shoulders in it's execution. The step is asymmetrical in nature with the passing step smaller than the recovered step.

Cross to the 90 - [Off-Line Step] A Cross stepping farther around the Star to the 90 degree line to either the right or left.

Cross to the Back 45 - [Off-Line Step] A Cross stepping deeper around the Star to the back 45 degree line to either the right or left.

Deep Lunge - (see Lunge)

> **DEFINITION**
>
> **Demi:** From Latin *dīmidium* ("divided in half"), via Old French and Middle English *demi-* ("half").

*****En Garde** - The basic "ready" position of a combatant..

Fléche - A running attack.

Fore - Abbreviation for "forward," generally used in footwork as in a Reprise to the "Fore."

Forward 45 - A specific line on an Imaginary Star that consists of 45-degree relationships to the primary North-South and East-West lines. The Forward 45 refers then to those lines of movement that would be to the North East and North West.

Forward 90 - A specific line on an Imaginary Star that consists of 45-degree relationships to the primary North-South and East-West lines. The Forward 90 refers then to those lines of movement that would be to the North. This is also the Line of Engagement.

Half Passe Back - The action of bringing the forward foot back to the rear foot in preparation to take a 2nd step

    For the 2nd half you can either:
1. Change - Starting with a Half Passe, the feet change so that the rear foot kicks out, remains behind, or performs a Thwart, Cross or Slip.
2. Continue - Starting with a Half Passe and Continuing on with the same foot to finish in a Passe, Thwart, Cross or Slip.
3. Return - The back foot Returns to the original En Garde.

Half Passe Forward - The action of bringing the back foot up to the front foot in preparation to take a 2nd step.

    For the 2nd half you can either:
1. Change - Starting with a Half Passe, the feet change so that the forward foot kicks out, remains forward, and steps to either a linear step or a Traverse.
2. Continue - Starting with a Half Passe and continuing on with the same foot to finish in either a Passe or a Traverse.
3. Return - The back foot Returns to the original En Garde.

The actions of all Half-Passes and 2nd steps are performed in 2 counts; one-Half Passe, two-Continue, Change or Return.

Line of Engagement -
    a.) An imaginary line that represents the shortest distance between two combatants.
    b.) The imaginary line on the Star consisting of the Forward 90 and Back 90 that connects two combatants when in an En Garde position.

*****Lunge** - [Linear Step] The "extended" leg position used as a method of reaching the opponent on an attack. To Lunge, the leading leg extends forward in a long step, while the trailing leg stays in one place.
    Lunges are of 3 sizes: 1. Shallow (Demi)   2. Standard   3. Deep (Grande)

Narrow Stance - A sword bearing foot forward stance that places the feet straddling the line of engagement and the 90 right and left lines of the Star, keeping the feet almost heel to heel and allowing the upper body to either face the line of engagement, or turn away.

Off-Line - To be off or outside The Line of Engagement.

Off-Line Step - [Also Traverse] Any movement that takes the body away from the line of engagement.

On-Line - [Also Line of Engagement] To be on or inside the imaginary line that connects two combatants when in an En Garde position..

On-Line Step - [Also Linear Step] Any step that either moves forward or backward along the line of engagement.

*__Passe, Single__ - <u>Forward</u> - The placing of the rear foot in front of the leading foot.
(a walking step)
<u>Backward</u> - The placing or the front foot in back of the rear foot.

Passe, Double - The combination of 2 Passes, either both Forward, or both back.

Passe, Full - [linear Step] A type of Passe, forward or back, larger than a Crossover, that changes the alignment of the feet, hips and shoulders to a new En Garde in it's execution.

Passe, Full Double - [linear step] A type of Double Passe, forward or back, larger than a Double Crossover, that does not change the alignment of the feet, hips and shoulders in it's execution.

Passive Hand - A non-sword bearing arm/hand that is kept behind the body for balance and not used to attack or defend.

Pattinando - A combination of an Advance and a Lunge. There are two counts in this action; one-advance, two-lunge.

Posting Foot - The foot that stays stationary when performing a step.
<u>Posted step:</u>. A step where there is a posted foot. (One count)
Examples: Lunge, Passes Forward and Back, Posted Thwart, Cross, Slip,
Half-Passe, Continue, and Return

Recovered Foot - A foot that makes a recovery to En Garde after performing a step.
<u>Recovered step:</u> A step where the foot recovers.(two count)
Examples: Advance/Retreat, Recoveries Forward and Back from a Lunge
Recovered Thwart, Half-Passe, change

*__Recovery Forward__ - To arrive at an En Garde position from a lunge by bringing the rear foot forward.

*__Recovery Backward__ - To arrive at an En Garde position from a lunge by bringing the forward foot backward.

Reprise to the Fore - A combination of a Recovery Forward and a Lunge. There are two counts in this action, one-recover, two-lunge. The sword arm stays extended.

*__Retreat__ - The rear foot steps backward, followed by the front foot.

Return - See Half Passe

*__Slip__ - A Posted circular step Traversing to the <u>Back</u> 45-degree line, taking the body Off - Line to either the right or left and ending with the legs crossed.

> **Angelo Slip** – A Slip Right, which is preceded by a lateral step with the right foot to the right.

Slip to the 90 - A Slip stepping farther through to the 90 degree line to either the right or left. A specific type of Slip to the 90 <u>Right</u> is also called a Demi - Volte.

> ***Demi - Volte** - A method of effacing the target by swinging the rear leg backward and sideways, so that the trunk is brought 90 degrees in relation to the attack.

Slip to the Forward 45 - A Slip stepping deeper around the star to the forward 45-degree line to either the right or left.

    A specific type of Slip to the For. 45 <u>Right</u> is also called a Volte.

> ***Volte** - A method of effacing the target by swinging the rear leg backwards and sideways, so that the trunk is brought 180 degrees in relation to the attack.

Shallow Lunge - (see Lunge)

Stance - The foot positions and posture of the body that support the act of being En Garde.

Standard Step - a). The established middle landmark for any step within the structure of three sizes of steps: Shallow, Standard and Deep.
b). The neutral execution of any step.

Standard Lunge - (see Lunge)

Standing Lunge - A leaning forward from En Garde without any forward foot movement and that recreates the parameters of a lunge: back leg straight, forward knee over ankle etc.

Star - An imaginary series of 8 lines on the floor that radiate out from a central apex, beneath the combatant, consisting of 45 degree relationships like the points of a compass or lines of an apex. The points of the star indicate the variable planes of movement that a combatant can take.

*Thwart - A Posted or Recovered Traverse on the <u>Forward</u> 45 degree line, taking the body Off - Line to either the right or left and ending with the legs open.

Thwart to the 90 - A Thwart stepping farther around the Star to the 90 degree line to either the right or left.

Thwart to the Back 45 - A Thwart stepping deeper around the star to the back gf45-degree line to either the right or left.

Transitional Step - Any step that is part of a larger whole, but has a definite beginning and end: Usually has multiple options at its completion.
    Example: The first half of an Avance or Reatreat.

*Traverse - Any foot movement that takes the combatant Off - Line.

Wide Stance - An En Garde that places the feet wide apart and allows the upper body to face the line of engagement.
   Feet may either be: <u>Neutral</u> (feet on 90 left and 90 Right)
                       <u>Right foot forward</u> (right foot on the forward 45 right, left foot on back 45 left)
                       <u>Left foot forward</u> (Left foot on forward 45 left and back foot on back 45 left)

Appendix 1

Proximity:
The consequences of distance while in conflict.

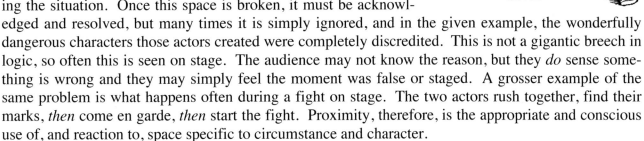

Two characters enter the stage. They are obviously at odds with one another. They look dangerous; at any moment they might fly into violence. Suddenly, one offends the other and they dash towards each other, stopping face to face with fists clenched and eyes staring. What happens next? The script and director did not have a fight planned so what happens? Unfortunately, the actors separated themselves from this overly tight staging as an afterthought and disengaged leaving the audience wondering if they missed something.

This conflict illustrates a common problem in today's theatre; a lack of understanding and respect for proximity. It can manifest itself in subtle or gross ways. In the example given, the two characters violently invaded the personal space of the other, while ignoring the changes in life both characters must experience if they do so and, once there, exited the same space without resolving the situation. Once this space is broken, it must be acknowledged and resolved, but many times it is simply ignored, and in the given example, the wonderfully dangerous characters those actors created were completely discredited. This is not a gigantic breech in logic, so often this is seen on stage. The audience may not know the reason, but they *do* sense something is wrong and they may simply feel the moment was false or staged. A grosser example of the same problem is what happens often during a fight on stage. The two actors rush together, find their marks, *then* come en garde, *then* start the fight. Proximity, therefore, is the appropriate and conscious use of, and reaction to, space specific to circumstance and character.

This essay shall examine the various aspects of personal space and will apply specific parameters to reactions. The goal is to find a truthful process for the actor to discover appropriate reactions to space and distance both in and out of conflict. It is divided into four parts:
1. An examination of the actors own personal space, and how that space is defined through circumstance
2. An examination of governors: time, proportion, judgment; These parameters shall help define a vocabulary for appropriate and inappropriate reactions to circumstance giving the actor an active choice in the moment
3. Putting attributes into action
4. Putting the actions into a process of discovery in rehearsal

Some are born close, some achieve closeness, and some have closeness thrust upon 'em.

Shakespeare (sort of) 1601

The amount of personal space people allow in their life varies. The amount they demand might be reasonable and healthy for personal interaction or may be destructive. People exist that are of a generous spirit who allow others to be close very easily and there they are comfortable. Other individuals live in fear; anger or hurt and so have a place in their heart, circumstances in their life and their surrounding space where no one may enter. Everyone has met these people; extreme examples are seen daily on tabloid television shows. Either choice of lifestyle has its advantages, disadvantages and consequences; a generous person might easily allow intimacy, but openness to the point of naiveté put some in a position to be hurt. Another person who has experienced much hurt in their life may wisely protect themselves, but one who holds on to and lives in that hurt pushes any chance of intimacy away from them. Keith Johnston in his book "Impro" discusses the power of status and the choices an actor may make: "Suddenly we understood that every inflection and movement implies a status, and that no action is due to chance, or really motiveless.[3]" This awareness addresses the very core of a character and is as important as other, more obvious, details like a dialect or the way a person walks: and so each person would respond differently to a proclamation of love, an act of violence, *or how another character enters and leaves their space*.

Exercise 1*
"Finding Your Own Space"
*This exercise was inspired by similar work done by Colleen Kelly[4]

It is imperative that these exercises be done slowly to allow all impulses to be felt and acted upon.

I. Establish partners and designate who is "**X**" and "**Y**"

II. **X** stands on one side of a room, while **Y** stands on the opposite side. Slowly walk toward each other and simply remain open and acknowledge when it feels the partner is beginning to enter into what feels like personal space. This could be at any distance. Keep walking until both are about one foot apart. Take time and try this a few times.
People Watching - Is the moment where both of X and Y hit an invisible wall apparent? Do the participants acknowledge that moment? What happens as they continue in?

III. While continuing to walk in together, **X** will stop where it feels to be a comfortable place. **Y** will continue into the space until they are about one foot apart. Do this a few times and switch.
People Watching - How does it feel to see someone stop while the other walks into the space? What sort of story does this simple action say? Describe the reactions of each participant at the moment of closure.

IV. This time, both **X** and **Y will** stop when they feel they have reached a place where they are comfortable. Try not to impose circumstance - only acknowledge the instinctual, natural impulse to stop.

---

[3] Impro: Improvisation and the Theatre by Keith Johnstone. Theatre Arts Books 1989
[4] Colleen Kelly is an SAFD Fight Director and head of movement / resident Fight Director at The Alabama Shakespeare Festival.

People watching - Is one side inadvertently acting "tough" and not stopping just to continue in? Do both stop at the same time? One might be more comfortable closer than the other. Did one side in fact want to stop but did not do so because the other person was still going? What feelings are experienced when one stops and the other keeps walking? Was there mutual agreement or invitation? Did one side barrel through the other's personal bubble? What does this simple action say?

The goal is to work on a mutual stopping point with which both are comfortable. Stay there for a few moments then mutually decide to disengage.
People watching - How is this space agreed upon? Is the negotiation apparent?

V. After discovering an agreed upon space, walk to it and stop. Then, one side decide to break it by walking in further. Eventually stand nose to nose. What are the feelings? If one side felt threatened, at what point did this happen? One foot? Three feet? Is there, in fact, no feeling of being threatened but of being comfortable? Be honest.
People watching - How do these people pass through each of the closer spaces of intimacy?

While watching these exercises, note what different techniques people use to get inside space and communicate their feelings. Each person will bring their own unique history to the work, and although actors train to be a sort of "empty vessel", or "neutral" in the work, understanding ourselves is a necessary first step towards making any active choices to the contrary.

Exercise 2
"Adding Circumstance"

I. In this exercise, while keeping in mind that there is no imposing of character outside of the participants own personality, imagine now that the partner is a stranger.
   a. It is a lonely street at night. How do things change?
   b. Change environments - A bank, the subway. Include more people and turn it into a birthday party filled with good friends, then a busy city street, then a funeral.

Two general rules are discovered:

II. Two bubbles of personal space exist: An outside, or larger bubble, which informs about the environment and situation and a second bubble much closer to the body that is truly personal space.
   a. This essay will classify this "larger" bubble as not necessarily personal space but a "sphere of influence" where a person may be aware of someone near, but in most societies, the proximity is on an acceptable level.

III. The size of personal space depends on the environment. Is it a place that is safe or dangerous? Do friends or enemies populate it? If safe, the garde is down and the individual is open for interaction. If dangerous, the garde is up and interaction is limited.
   a. In certain environments (the city, a crowded subway) it is acceptable for people to exist inside personal space because of sociological necessity or circumstance. Here, we as individuals agree to allow people into personal space, but under specific rules such as; no talking, no eye contact. If these rules are broken without careful permission politely asked, then guards go up.

Once the individual has an understanding of their own space and are open to some of the many changes inherent in it, the next exercises will begin to put direct, applicable structure to this awareness. This will begin with an examination of what a neutral, trained fighter might look like, then how through specific choices, knowledgeably create a character.

He that is nearest, hitteth soonest
Giocomo di Grassi 1594

In any acting "technique" there needs to be structure; visual and emotional understanding of the consequences to an action. Exploration through improvisation and scene study to the point of mastery frees the student from the shackles of that structure and eventually leads to freedom of expression. Just as a student of painting must first learn the *craft* of painting, (strong performance parameters imposed upon that student as a particular path that the teacher, through their knowledge, has determined must be followed) before moving on to a personal style, so must an actor learn appropriate choices for situations of conflict before they are expected to knowledgeably make the choice to follow or break them because of a theatrical circumstance.

If one actor on stage tells another that they are loved, that actor must then draw from their emotional experience to make an appropriate circumstantial choice in reaction. In order to do this, the actor must have a foundational emotional availability, and all schools of acting have specific exercises to explore and develop this awareness. Through this availability, the actor builds a veritable encyclopedia of language both verbal and non-verbal to tell the story of their love, and it is this range of choice that defines a strong and versatile actor. In conflict, the actor needs to clearly understand the concept of physical proximity and all the associated consequences. Then they must have the movement and vocal based vocabulary to tell a varied and interesting story with many "words" at their disposal.

Unfortunately most actors, although they might be emotionally available, do not have extensive experience with physical conflict let alone sword fighting. Their practical "emotional" knowledge of conflict and distance that they may be able to draw upon is severely limited. Outside of actors who have experience in the martial arts or fencing, the extent of understanding the concept of *en garde* might be; "if they can reach me, they can hit me". The vocabulary available to these actors for use in telling this very complex story is, therefore, with only one or two "words", severely limiting the possibilities of the scene. To address this, we must create a structure for the actor who is inexperienced in conflict to begin to visualize and react appropriately, as a trained fighter would, to proximity. Then they need to explore choices in those circumstances to increase the actor's vocabulary so that they are actively choosing what "word" to use from moment to moment.

Governors: or, What Makes a Good Fighter.

Most people, who try to describe what a trained fighter looks like, usually end up sounding like that supreme court justice who said: "I don't know how to define pornography, but I know it when I see it." This is very true: the audience can tell when actors do not understand the nature of defending themselves in a correct manner. We can, however, briefly discuss specific attitudes and reaction modes that give the actor a starting point for understanding appropriate reactions while *en garde*[5]. When reactions match the distance of the moment, then the illusion works.

All fighters from all fighting styles have ways, names and philosophies to describe what one must do to stay protected while *en garde*. This essay uses certain phrases from 16th and 17th century fight masters because the belief is that they best convey specific images helpful to the actor, and *the author has taken his own interpretations for use in these acting exercises.*

Elizabethan masters of defense called attributes one can bring to defense, and more specifically for our purposes, *en garde* **governors**. Vincentio Saviolo writing in 1595 called them **distance**, **time** and **proportion**; George Silver, Giocomo di Grassi, Joseph Swetnam, and other Elizabethan era masters, used words such as: **distance**, **time**, **place** and **judgment**. Balancing these governors (like balancing the humors to insure good health) ensures victory. **Distance** will continue to be examined in this essay, but now we will take a moment to define **time**, **judgment** and **proportion** and explore these three ways for a fighter to balance the many instant decisions one must make while *en garde*.

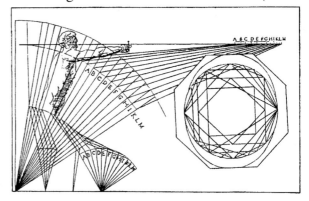

Agrippa - 1568

TIME

To take time, is to say when opportunity is proffered you, either by his lying unregarded or upon your enemy's profer, then make a quick answer, I mean it must be done upon the very motion of his profer, you must defend and seek to offend all at once, for you must not suffer your enemy to recover his guard, for if you do, you loose your advantage.

Joseph Swetnam 1617

---

[5] *The Society of American Fight Directors defines en garde* in their glossary of terms as: "the basic ready position for sword fighters". One may be "on their guard", however, in many different situations, so *en garde* will be used universally in this essay to describe the action of being prepared for conflict.

Time is doing the appropriate thing at the appropriate moment. To parry when it is time to parry, to attack when it is time to attack. When an effective fighter is described, it is said that he has good **timing**. For now, think of this as rhythm. A good fighter will try to control their opponent's rhythm: One way is to lull them into their own rhythm in order to get them into a predictable way of moving. They then take advantage of that rhythm by doing a move on a syncopated beat (a half beat, quarter beat etc.). While actors do not need to beat their partner to the punch, they *do* need to show the audience how an opening is created and the advantage taken. One tool is **time**.

Exercise 3
"Changing the Rhythm"

I. Pick **X** and **Y** and face each other. **X** will have the job of lightly touching **Y** on either shoulder out near the arm. **Y**'s job is to defend with his arms the touch. Both begin a slow jog in place. **X** should match **Y**'s rhythm. *Without changing this rhythm*, attempt to touch **Y** when the feet touch the floor (on the beat). Be sure to avoid the face. It will be discovered that it is very hard to succeed in making a touch. At first, attempt to touch on every beat, then pick randomly. It will still not matter when the choice to touch the partner happens if on the beat because **Y** will know exactly the **time** in which the touch will happen.

II. Continue on as before, but change two things.
   a. Try to touch off the beat
   b. Vary the length of time between touches. It will be found to be easier to touch **Y** on the arm. Continue to make the rhythm more unpredictable, changing into half beats, quarter beats, etc. If **Y** is still successful in blocking the touch, try lulling them into a rhythm and then quickly and forcefully change it on the touch. *By forcefully is meant to do it quickly, efficiently and with total commitment to the moment and performance to the action but not in a heavy or unthoughtful manner.*

III. The next step, after liberal switching back and forth, is to play with both sides simultaneously. Be careful not to try for a hit, but instead, provide stimuli to each other and react by being true to the timing of the moment - listen to each other. What will be discovered is that conscious control of the rhythm can be a very effective tool in beating someone to the punch.

Time is one important visual tool that can be brought to the work of *en guard*. Understanding the power of controlling rhythm may provide a new way to look at Mohammed Ali and what, in fact, he was doing. Some people will mimic changes in rhythm because they saw a boxer do it once, but the rhythm very often is vague and not specific in response to a partner and the circumstance of the moment. Therefore, the appropriate application for changes in rhythm is called **time**, or "finding your **time**". This will become a foundational attribute to all the skills and exercises to follow.

PROPORTION

This ward truly is very good against all other wards in my opinion, especially if you knew how to charge your enemy, & to find time & proportion to strike knowing how to turn and shift your body as well on the one side as the other, and understanding the skill of fight, and being most nimble, you may answer him with it.

Vincentio Saviolo 1595

Proportion, used in this essay, is where and how the body is placed in space, and, ultimately, how it reacts to distance. Is the body balanced, mobile and protected with the arms, legs or the weapon? Or is the body out of balance, immobile and open? Transitions from one position to another are done with understanding of open and closed line, balanced stances and rhythmatic independence. If the choice is to invite an attack by consciously leaving open a target or line, it is done judiciously and with the understanding of the consequences. The very word: **Proportion** conveys a sense of spatial awareness and line of the body.

Finding ones "center" is a cornerstone of most stage combat programs as well as training in the martial arts. The goal is to allow the body to move together as a unit: arms, legs and torso - supported and sustained by the center of gravity, in a relaxed yet focused way. A combination of breathing, balance and slow sustained movement exercises develop this power and practicing this over a number of years gives the serious student the appearance of someone who is confident and in control whether standing, fighting or *en garde*. Studying in this way is, of course, the best path. But for those who need to create this illusion without years of martial study, the following exercises will help the novice understand the basics.

Exercise 4*
"Control the Triangle"
*This exercise was inspired by similar work done by Greg Dolph[6]

I. X and Y face each other. X's job will be to unbalance Y. Y will stand in a simple neutral open stance with both feet even and shoulders width apart. X must find the angles where the balance is strongest and weakest. In this stance, it will be found that Y is best balanced from side to side but most vulnerable forward and back. Push Y enough so that balance is lost backwards and they are forced to take a step. What happens? In order to stop the imbalance, Y has stepped not just back on one foot, but close to a central line which bisects the body while standing in neutral. The posted foot and the two positions of the moving foot form a triangle. What Y has just done is change their stance according to the circumstance (the push) to maintain balance. Y has also changed the angle X must push in order to achieve an imbalance. Without changing the previous angle (straight on) try now pushing Y after this step - it will be much harder to unbalance Y because the feet are now in line with the push. Push harder. What happens? Y must deepen their stance, establish a wider base and create a lower center of gravity.

II. Now X will attempt to unbalance Y by pushing on what appears to be the weakest angle. Y's job is to step in an appropriate way to stay in balance. What ends up happening? In order to get to an advantageous angle, X must circle around. Y forms a series of one foot forward stances in order to focus energy in a linear way towards X, equalizing the force placed on them by using the triangle. Also, it will be discovered that X is creating their own triangles to serve their objectives. Vary the strength of the push; as in the earlier exercise Y must now vary the deepness of their step in response.

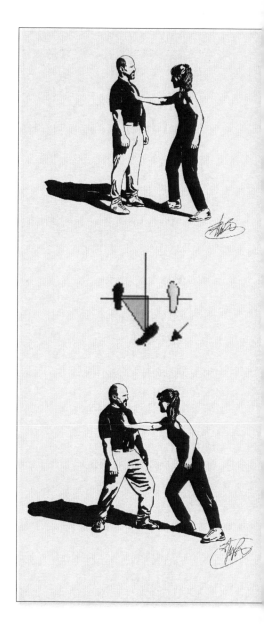

III. With the information discovered so far from this exercise, do the same thing from a greater distance without making physical contact. As both circle, X is attempting to find a moment where Y's triangle is vulnerable, and using **time**, rush in and threaten that balance. Meanwhile, Y changes the angle and positioning of their feet to best protect their balance, while at the same time, stepping back deep and lowering their center enough to match the implied attacking energy. No real contact should be made. Both X and Y should keep their arms out and away from the body, as if the arms would cushion any potential impact, while exploring what angles the arms can provide to protect the body from someone coming in to push them.

---

[6] Greg Dolph is an actor and fight director in the Los Angeles area.

IV. After liberal switching of roles, practice both attack and defense at once. What has now developed are two individuals circling themselves in search of something specific: control of their partner's balance. They are now using an understanding of balance and angle, while using **time** to take advantage of a moment of vulnerability. While defending, they are also using balance and angle in **proportion** when it comes to stepping deeply enough on the triangle: deep enough to keep balance against the assault, yet not so deep as to lose mobility. Also, both are using **time**: not to be lulled into a rhythm but keeping the rhythm unpredictable. Both are learning to use **time** and **proportion** together *in* **proportion**.

This is what two fighters would be doing while *en garde*: searching for openings, angles of attack and places where one may take the balance of the other, then changing or controlling rhythm in order to take advantage of that opening.

Another aspect of **proportion** is how the body and all the parts are held while *en garde*. It is not enough to understand rhythm and angle if the body is out of balance and either too stiff or too loose. Through the previous exercises, we now understand how to keep the feet and hips in **proportion** to maintain balance against an outside force; but what about the body remaining in balance (and looking so) while in a neutral *en garde*? What about the arms and legs: how can they contribute to the illusion? Once again, years of martial training brings people to this place, but through some exercises we might get an idea of this dynamic.

Exercise 5
"Using the Arms"

I. Using exercise four as a basis, **X** will once again attempt to unbalance **Y**. This time **X** will hold **Y**'s wrists. Attempt to unbalance **Y** in two ways:
  a. **Y** will stand in a neutral stance with arms straight out and locked.
   Push or pull the arms.
   What happens?
   What moves first?
With a jolt, the upper body does: it has no choice.
  b. **Y** will tightly press their arms against their chest and **X** will push or pull them again.
   Now what?
   Same thing.
The upper body has no choice in the movement because the arms cannot inform and guard against the movement dictated, and **Y** loses their balance.

II. This time, hold the arms out about two thirds of the way extended in a relaxed but firm way. Once again, push and pull. What happens now? **Y** now has a substantial amount of time that their body can react to the push or pull. This is because the arms can now inform about the direction of the energy before they collapse into the body or lock out. This allows your body to step forward, back or to the side in a controlled and balanced way before the upper body is forced into any direction. With the arms balanced energy wise - not too full (or stiff) and not to relaxed (or loose), the arms provide much information.

III. Now, start in earnest: **X** holding **Y**'s wrists and trying all sorts of angles to unbalance them, and **Y** stepping in an appropriate way to maintain balance while using the arms as an early warning device. If the energy in the arms are too loose, there will be a whiplash like effect that works against **Y**. On the other extreme, if **Y**'s arms are too stiff, they act as a lever; and the same thing happens; by the time the information of the push or pull is processed, it is too late to react in **proportion**. Start by lightly pushing while changing angles. Both will start moving together: one providing the stimulus and the other reacting. Be true to the angle and be kind to your partner as both become comfortable with the exercise and begin playing with more energy.

*Remember: if either X or Y's arms get too stiff, lighten up the exercise. Try not to fight with our partner, but instead, continually provide a safe environment for discovery then challenge their new technique in **proportion** to their performance.*

IV. Continue this exercise allowing **Y** to let their arms play a larger role in deflecting the energy of the push. With a pair of coordinated, energized, yet relaxed arms, **Y** will start to feel **X**'s energy and deflect it in an appropriate way. Examine this moment. Where does **Y**, in deflecting the energy of **X** take their arms? Do they go high or low? Do the arms collapse into the body? It will be found that, to be most effective, **Y** will deflect **X**'s arms away to the side and down into their center of gravity - this would be the safest area to take the arms in order to maintain balance. In other words, if **Y** allowed their arms above the head, or close into their body, then **Y** would find themselves out of **proportion** and off balance.

    A. Examine how effectively **Y** can deflect **X**'s energy. There is a window of opportunity where **Y** may easily deflect the push, but if **Y** is too early or too late, they must use much more energy to attain the same result. This window is their **time**. Once you "find your **time**", perceptually there is much more time to perform any given task; almost as if time slows down.

    B. Examine the angles of both the body and the arms spatially in relation to the partner: which arm is forward, which leg is back and why. This will become the basis of any *en garde* stance. Each time **X** moves circularly around the guard of **Y**, and **Y** changes their angle to guard their balance; the body has a leading and trailing foot, shoulder and arm. This is defined by the triangle **Y** is attempting to maintain.
      a. Try making the forward shoulder have a trailing arm. Does this feel natural? You would be out of **proportion** as the body twists around to bring the arm into play.

V. Now, like in exercise four, separate a few feet and do the same thing except with no contact. **Y** should have their arms out and extended in order to supply information and ward **X** off. As **X** circles around or diminishes distance linearly, **Y** must step back and maintain **proportion** using **time** to give themselves the time to perform the adjustment. Just as the feet should never be caught in a neutral stance or inactive, neither should the hands. They are in constant motion in relationship with the body, angle and rhythm.

It is now time to specify a simple generic **en garde** stance that should be used as a basis to balance the **governors** in the illusion we are creating. The legs have been defined but what about the arms? In the previous exercises, we saw how the arms must be active, but the question is; where is a good place to put them?

Exercise 6
"Establishing en garde"

I. For now, always keep the same forward arm and leg. If the left leg is forward, then so should the left arm. It is extended but not locked out. The other arm is placed back at the depth of the extended arms elbow (half way out and half way in). The elbows are bent and tucked inside, not protruding outside the line of the body.

    a. Consider the forward arm as an antennae or "asking hand". It is out there to provide information about the partner (especially if in contact). Think of the trailing hand as the "protecting hand". If something gets through the asking hand, then the protecting hand is able to pick it up.

II. Change guards from right foot forward to left foot forward. Step forward or back maintaining the same angle. During this transition the arms and legs must move together. Practice smooth transitions from one side to the other.

    a. Vary the deepness of step and be sure to keep the arm moving in proportion with the leg

    b. Vary the angle in 45-degree increments. From a right foot forward stance, step to the left with the left leg on a 45 degree angle. Then try a 90-degree transition.

III. Apply this new awareness of *en garde* to the exercises previous. After switching back and forth from reacting to, and providing the stimuli, the next step again is to do both simultaneously.

    a. Imagine you in conflict with your partner; the stakes are very high; perhaps your life is at stake. Even though you will not actually throw a punch, explore all the possibilities of this dynamic situation. The reason for this is so this exploration of the danger is made honestly; not in a Cavalier fashion.

What is now seen are two bodies that are balanced with a stable yet mobile base, arms that are out and inquisitive, with rhythm and angles that are either continually changing in response to the stimuli of the other, or attempting to control the same. This is the dialogue that happens with two fighters that are *en garde* and these are the first steps to showing this illusion on stage. If the two actors are truly listening to each other and responding appropriately given these basic parameters, then, on a basic level, the illusion will be that they are in conflict and responding wisely to the other.

...through Time you safely win or gain the Place of your adversary, the Place being won or gained you have timed safely either to strike, thrust, ward, close, grype, slip or go back, in the which time your enemy is disappointed to hurt you   Joseph Swetnam 1617

Place is a moment in time where advantage can be taken. "Gaining the place" means that one person has put themselves into position (defined by **distance**, **time** and **proportion**) where they may strike and, in the most successful cases, the other person cannot. This is the ultimate goal in the simplistic scene that has been created for this examination - it is not enough to get away with a hit and being hit also, but in a life or death struggle, to get a hit and be able to get out of the situation safely; anything else is a modification of this simple circumstance; a Cavalier attitude to the danger and what we see much too often on stage.

...through Judgment, you keep your distance...
George Silver 1599

With these attributes - **time**, **place**, **proportion** and the specific goals that come with them in terms of being *en garde*, **judgment** is about reacting appropriately at a given time given the circumstances (ie) **distance** of the moment, **proportion** of your body and the partners, modified through **time** in order to find your **place**.

...through Distance you take your Time
George Silver 1599

As in many martial philosophies, things come full circle and each **governor** informs the other. If one **governor** is out of **proportion** in any of its definitions, one is vulnerable. Then **judgment** informs what must be done based on **distance**.

there is a Time and Place for that....
My Mother 1969

Now that there has been an examination of the attributes that create the illusion of **governors**, it is time to get more specific about **distance**, since this will now be the most variable of the **governors** and how the other **governors** are judged.

The Three Rings

These three rings represent **distance** and the changing dynamic that must accompany any transition from one to the other. The type of fight dictates the distance and the size of these rings. An unarmed fight is gauged by arm and leg length. In a sword fight, all three rings would be larger to reflect the extended reach.

When appropriate reactions are mentioned in these exercises, it is with the understanding that both participants are working within the basic parameters discussed in earlier chapters (trained fighters dealing straightforwardly with a situation and keeping their **governors** in balance) without adding anything else.

1st Ring - At this distance the two partners are within easy striking distance. A punch, kick or push could easily land with very little change in distance, perhaps leaning in of the body. This would be similar to the distance of two boxers while they exchange blows, or lunging distance while swordfighting. The garde is up and the actors are aware of, and respond *immediately* to, any movement their partner performs. The stakes and danger are at their highest. **Time** here is very short. One cannot spend much time at this distance before something must happen. It is also very difficult to retreat from this circle without a character loosing face.

2nd Ring - At this distance, one side must make a large move in order to strike the other, such as a passe forward into a lunge, or a crossover step to kick. There is more **time** here. The garde is more relaxed than in the first ring, but still is "connected". Neither partner can afford to drop their garde completely, look or turn away. At this distance fatigue and injury may be invested, but very carefully.

This is where most of the the character *en garde* "testing" takes place or were a Guardia is held. One may stay here longer than the first circle, but eventually something must happen.

3rd Ring - At this distance, neither partner can hit the other without taking a few steps inward. The garde can safely be more relaxed. This is the distance to drop the garde for a quick moment to catch a breath or invest in an injury. From this distance, looking away has much more latitude, the garde may be broader and the movements bigger because a trained fighter would know what it would require, and how much **time** it would take for the opponent to traverse the given distance. This is not to say that they are not *en garde*; if the partner diminishes distance the response should be immediate, but there is simply more latitude in terms of the **governors** because the **time** it would take an opponent to traverse the distance will allow the person who is *en garde* the **time** to find their **proportion** before they are endangered.

Anything outside this third ring is completely out of distance, but still in a "sphere of influence", and a trained fighter would know that this circumstance could change at any time and must be acknowledged. Outside the third circle would be a place for a person to escape to during a fight to in order to rest or have dialogue. This is the space to invest in an injury or turn away for whatever reason. The more **distance** away from the third circle, the more **time** the individual has, and the less **proportion** is needed to maintain an *en garde*.

This is the very crux of the matter and, although this last paragraph seems to have stated the obvious, what we see much to often on stage. Two fighters separating and perhaps resting, going to one knee or some other position that is not *en garde* but too close to be believable. Sometimes actors are asked to take this kind of acting beat within the second circle - and sometime in the first!

Exercise 7
"Exploring the Three Rings"

In an unarmed situation, begin exploring the rings. Establish an *en garde*, *but do not launch into an attack* - just keep the *en garde* in balance and experience the changes from one circle to the other. Still, at this point, try not to make any choices in character or circumstance - only that the reactions are grounded in the basic way explored earlier. This is a chance to balance the **governors** and explore wise and judicious decisions for the moment.

1. <u>Explore the first ring</u>. Reactions to each other should be immediate and focused. Feel the intensity. Everyone participating will quickly feel that they must either commit forward into an attack or back away from this first circle. In other words, there is very little **time** in which to react to an attack. This also means one might overreact (loss of **proportion**) to a false attack (feint[7]) and both participants rhythms become very "brittle" with one, or both going out of control. Either way, it is not a comfortable **place** in which to be. Ones **proportion** is very important here in terms of "keeping your guard up". If moving around the circle, try to maintain the distance.
    a. Take turns giving feints (improvisational offers) to each other in order to supply something with which to react. Be sure that only one side is giving the stimuli at this point. In reacting to a feint, maintain **proportion** or else an opening is created. If a feint is performed and the partner looses **proportion** does the other recognize it?

2. <u>Explore the second ring</u>: One person take a large step backward. Discover the second ring and how it feels to live there. While moving either linearly or in a circle, try to keep the distance consistent.
    a. After having explored this distance, stay *en garde* and one side slowly enter into the first ring and see what happens. Go back and forth from the first to the second ring without attacking, simply experiencing the changes in garde.

---

[7] A feint, or feint attack is defined be The Society of American Fight Directors in their glossary of terms as: "Any attacking action deliberately intended not to land on a target. The aim is to draw a reaction or a parry."

3. <u>Explore the third ring:</u> Take another step back from the second circle and discover the third circle. How do things change? Maintain distance while circling.
    a. Now change between the third and second circle. Feel the *en guard* relaxing when backing into the third circle. What are the parameters of each persons **proportion** and how do they change?

    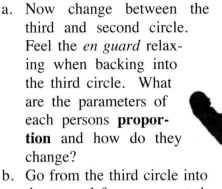

    b. Go from the third circle into the second for a moment then continue to the first. What changes as distance closes?
    c. As awareness of the rings, and the partner's reach develop, concentrate on **time** and **proportion**. Now, all three circles are available to play within; giving a chance for each to react in very specific ways by balancing the **governors**.

For simplicity sake, divide the responsibilities and have **X** provide stimuli while **Y** reacts so that there is no danger of collisions and gross overbalance of **governors**. Stay with that restriction for now. Go even farther and create a very simple circumstance having **Y** react to distance while having **X** aggressively change distance, always keeping in mind (especially **X**) that they are trying to keep their **governors** in balance. Switch roles liberally.

REVIEW

Review the **governors** while *en garde* and what dynamics each are trying to create for the illusion: how does **X** go about looking for and/or creating openings in **Y**'s defense and what **Y** is doing to stop any implied attack.

Partner who is diminishing Distance. (**X**)
1. Working **time** so they "get the jump" on **Y**, and diminishing distance before **Y** can react. They do this by finding a moment in **Y**'s rhythm and balance (**time** and **proportion**) where they are committed to an action and cannot react immediately.
2. Working angles - finding or creating the moment **Y** is out of **proportion** so they can unbalance them.
3. Maintaining their own **proportion** so they may have the **time** to take advantage of that split second **Y** is not. Also, so when they do rush in, they do not leave themselves open.

Partner who is reacting. (**Y**)
1. Reacting in the appropriate **Time** to either stop the implied attack and/or change garde because of a new distance and/or angle
2. When stepping, or changing their garde, staying in **proportion** in order to be both stable and mobile and never allowing a moment were they are off balance, or allowing a line to be open.

Questions:

Participants:
1. How long do you feel you can stay in the first circle before something must happen? Why is this?
2. How long can you stay in the 2nd. or 3rd. rings?
3. Without stopping the momentum of the garde - where can you best express yourself?

Observers:
1. Can you tell when false or inappropriate responses to stimuli are performed? How would you describe what you see?
2. Are the participants being completely neutral during the exercise (simply keeping their **governors** in balance), or are character choices starting to creep in? What defines a character choice in this circumstance?

STRATEGY

"So soon as ever thou seest him, draw; and as thou drawst, swear horrible; for it comes to pass oft that a terrible oath, with a swaggering accent sharply twanged off, gives manhood more approbation than ever proof itself would have earned him"

Sir Toby - Twelfth Night 1601

This section will briefly discuss different choices for an actor when developing the "dialogue" of *en garde*. A trained fighter would understand and apply the concepts discussed earlier, and this might make for a very competent and balanced fight, but there are still many dynamic choices a fighter may bring to a fight that does not "unbalance" their **governors**. This could be seen as characterization, but let's consider these, for now, wise and informed dynamics, for these are ways to flavor an *en garde* yet not break the rules set up earlier. This will take into account wise and judicious philosophies and strategies of fighting.

Agent and Patient

A well-trained and intuitive fighter can be aggressive and/or defensive in nature. Another word for these dynamics would be, according to George Silver; **Agent** and **Patient**. These are very appropriate words for the spirit of approaching an *en garde* situation. An **agent** fighter will be active: pressing for reactions of the other in order to set up an attack or gain information on their opponent. A **patient** fighter will wait for the other to commit to a movement or attack and react appropriately. Both type of fighters, if well trained, would keep all **governors** in balance, taking into consideration how close they are to the other (**distance**) and what information has been gathered while being *en garde*: Every move would have a **time** and **place**. In terms of story, it would show one fighter actively pressing for reactions while the other reacts appropriately waiting for a mistake to happen. Of course, in a perfectly balanced fight, this could go on forever.

A basic philosophy found throughout the martial arts and fencing is "when you attack, whether it is real attack or a false attack (a feint), you are at your most vulnerable". The **agent** fighter by the very nature of pressing for reactions leaves themselves open. They are taking chances in order to gain important information about their opponent. This strategy may begin small, and if the partner does not notice, react or take the bait, the attacks and/or openings may become bigger and bigger until they become an **invitation**.

Invitations

An **invitation** is basically what it sounds like. The fighter is "inviting" the other to attack them. This may be done in a variety of ways, but they all involve creating a moment when they themselves are vulnerable. The hope is that their opponent will commit to an action so that they may "spring a trap" on them. This may be done quickly in the midst of a number of moves, or singularly bringing focus to it.

An **agent** fighter, and this specific strategy: **invitation** should not be confused with more extreme character choices like cockiness or untrained arrogance, it is a specific tactic done for specific reasons. A **patient** fighter might also make **invitations**, but this would be done with much more subtlety, albeit for the same strategic reasons. An **invitation**, therefore, is a valuable tool in specifying or justifying how and why a first attack is made.

Exercise 8
"Be thine own Agent and Patient"

Go back to the earlier exercises of balancing the **governors** in relation to *the three rings of progression*, but now with the specific duty to explore being **agent** or **patient**. For now, be either fully **agent** or fully **patient**, and take turns being one or the other.

Eventually, any good fighter will be both **agent** and **patient** at any given moment. These dynamics would switch instantaneously back and forth, first **agent** pressing for reactions or openings and then **patient** laying in wait for a misjudgment, leaving their opponent wondering what will be happening next. The very nature of a *feint* attack is to be, at one instant, **agent** as you indicate an attack, then **patient** as the partner either reacts to the offered move or does not. If the offer is taken and the partner "takes the bait", and momentarily losses **proportion**, then that fighter reacts appropriately and continues into an attack that takes advantage of that loss of **proportion**.

After liberal switching back and forth, try being both **agent** and **patient** together.

Adding Character Choices

So far, this essay has examined and specified how a well-trained fighter might be proportioned while establishing parameters on how one would react to stimuli. A system has been articulated to gauge ones balance, proportion and timing for the purpose of cleanly showing a simplified neutral character:

a martial artist (in whatever definition time wise or culturally) in action. This is only the first step in terms of an actor's job: to present a specific character in a specific circumstance. The actor must be able to choose to show an untrained fighter or one that is frightened. How can one know, if the character is more afraid or less trained, or, when a character is raising their garde too early given the circumstance? If one does not know when it is appropriate for a knowledgeable fighter to do so, how can one knowledgeably violate that rule?

Any system exists in order to allow participants to know when they are *breaking* the rules of that system. Therefore, now that some basic concepts and rules have been established, the next exercises will explore how one may break them for specific reasons. This will be done with choices based on character and circumstance.

Exercise 9
"Break the Rules"

Make some assumptions now about two characters working the three rings. One is trained and courageous, the other is frightened and untrained. What are some choices that might convey to an audience that one does not know what they are doing or that they are afraid?
1. Raising of the garde early or late
2. Lost or no **proportion**
3. Over expenditure of energy at inappropriate times
4. Overreaction to feints resulting in lose of **proportion**
5. Loss or no sense of **time** - startle reactions or rhythms that have no basis in the situation

Explore these and other inappropriate reactions keeping in mind the seriousness of the circumstance in order to stay out of the realm of comedy, which is a danger here. See what other inappropriate responses can be created - each time will be different depending on what the partner, who is portraying all the balance that has been worked on so far, gives in terms of an offer.

Putting it all Together

Improvisation and stage combat are usually mutually exclusive. It is taught that the last thing to do in a fight is to "be inspired", doing something outside of what has been already rehearsed. But improvisation can have a place in these exercises if it is acknowledged there is an organic response that an *en garde* requires to be truly effective. In the exercises so far, **X** and **Y** have already been improvising with each other. What is improvisation but listening to a partner, not negating any offer that is given you and continuing, or adding to, the scene? So, with specific parameters in terms of attack, improvisation can be a valuable tool in discovering the moments of a fight before and leading up to the moment of the first choreographed attack.
The challenge is:
1. Discovering how long the scene should last.
2. How to safely explore and develop *consistency* through specific choices.
3. Understanding when and how to enter into the choreography.

Exercise 10
"Create a Scene"

1. Start with a very simple scene: **X** enters into a space outside of the 3rd. ring from **Y**. A circling section, then an approach into closer distance leading to a single punch that **Y** avoids. Decide the following things:
    a. The location of the audience
    b. Where the scene will start, where will both participants enter into the choreography (usually when working from choreography, the first moment will be very specific in terms of placement and angle on the stage)
    c. Are you trained as a fighter or untrained? For now, the easier and cleaner choice is to begin with both **X** and **Y** competently balancing their **governors**.
2. Work out a specific opening move for the choreography: Make it easy - a punch with much latitude for error: perhaps a punch that is avoided. Rehearse only the punch and make sure there is a small cue to let **Y** know when **X** is coming, while **Y**'s avoidance is rehearsed and made consistent.
3. Now the beginning and end of the scene has been defined, all that is left is to explore the time between the opening moment and the explosion into the first (and only) move of the choreography. Here is the time for improvisation using the techniques discussed earlier to inform all moment-to-moment decisions.
    a. Try playing with the circles and really build up the stakes. Eventually work your way into the first circle and slowly and clearly go into the pre - choreographed opening move. Try it a few times and agree on some general choices about the pattern of the closure. As comfort and consistency build and the cue to punch is well established, start to explore the **time** of the punch and explode (figuratively speaking) into it. Form the piece so that there is a clear escalation into the final explosion - make sure moment happens in the first circle.
4. Continue to refine and make more specific the moments that are discovered while improvising from the opening of the scene to the punch. Be true to the distance of the moment and all the attached dynamics. Practice so that the punch eventually does explode out of the moment and first circle.
    a. What are the cues you are giving your partner?
    b. Is the punch getting through your partners defenses or are you attacking a closed line?
        i. Justify how the punch gets in without diminishing the other character.
    c. Be careful not to restrict the choices linearly; in other words if you enter into the first circle, you always have the option to back out of it! This can add dimension to the story that is being created.
5. Do the same scene as rehearsed, and once in the first circle, stay there a little too long.
    a. How does this feel?
    b. How does this look to the people watching?
    c. At what point does it become false?
6. Try doing the same scene, but instead of working into the first circle, do the punch from slightly farther away. Play with this for awhile and work toward doing the punch from the second circle.
    a. How is this different from punching from the first circle?

What has been developed is a process in which to explore that all-important moment before the first attack in an organic way. Whether the character is trained and balanced or untrained and unbalanced, using this exercise will help the actor discover the choices available and create a scene safely and effectively.

Exercise 11
"Going back to the beginning"

Now that there is a basic understanding of the concepts discussed in this essay, such as: the "sphere of influence," the **governors**, the three rings, and how to portray a person who is either trained or not trained in a martial spirit, go back to the situation at the beginning of this tome. Two characters have reached the point where they are going to approach each other with intent to do harm but, in the given circumstances, there is no fight.

1. Play the moment of closure, and walk in nose to nose. This is the first ring at its best and here anything could happen, but the parameters of the scene are to withdraw. How can this be done when so close to your partner? It is easy if one *submits* to the other, but harder if both want to maintain their integrity. How can both decide to withdraw from the situation without losing face?

2. Continue playing using all three rings and discover how distance can inform the circumstance and dynamics of this situation. Find out how much time each circle demands in order to reach a resolution. Also, discover what can be used in terms of the **governors**; **time** and **proportion** defined by your **distance** that empower or weaken you in that space.

What will be discovered is that the **governors** are useful here as well. As one character stands within another character's space, **time** and **proportion** can be used (or not used) to advantage. Being true to the **distance** of the moment will inform the other **governors** resulting in truthful reactions.

A good example of space, and its power, is to look at a king, queen or most effectively - a dictator - one whom everyone fears. The space that these people control is both defined and powerful and anyone who enters into that space, shows a clear sign of submission and respect. The Queen of England sitting on her throne clearly has control of her space, but when she is alone and intimate with a lover, or family member, her life and the way she relates to space are completely different. If playing a servant on stage, what then is the spatial relationship between the master verses another servant? If playing the master, how can the space be filed and and the servants controlled on stage merely by your presence.

With these exercises, a structure has been defined to help develop the "muscles" of **proximity**, and explore other aspects of character. Hopefully this work will allow the actor, inexperienced in actual conflict or martial training, to have more useful and appropriate choices available to them. Conversely, the actor trained in the tactical arts, where intentions are hidden, might discover what the audience and other actors must see in order to tell an interesting story and once again, have more useful and appropriate choices available. This essay, of course, is only a beginning, and this study could go on for many more pages (and I probably will) but for now, place this new awareness in all applications. I hope you find as much joy in specificity as I have using this technique.

Payson Burt 1997

Step Sizes at a Glance

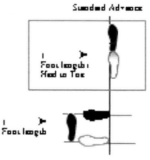
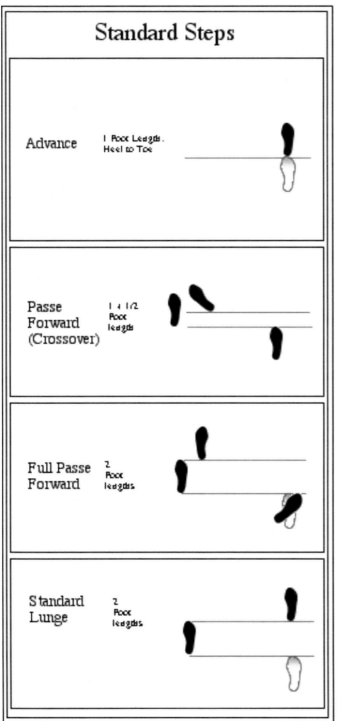
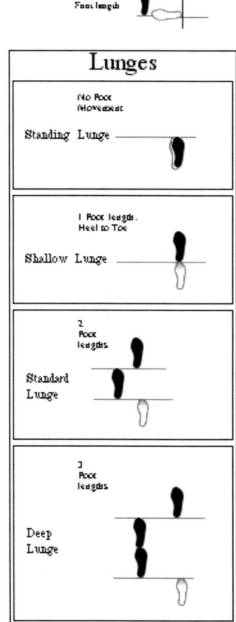

Made in United States
North Haven, CT
28 December 2021